MODEL SHIPS
from scratch

MODEL SHIPS
from scratch

Scott Robertson

NAVAL INSTITUTE PRESS, ANNAPOLIS, MARYLAND

First published in the UK by Argus Books 1994

Published and distributed in the United States of America and Canada by the
Naval Institute Press, 118 Maryland Avenue, Annapolis, Maryland 21402-5035.

Library of Congress Catalog Card Number 93-87265

ISBN 1-55750-589-6

Printed and bound in Great Britain.

Dedication

To my grandchildren Fiona, Ross, Guy and Scott.
They watch me working sometimes but are not allowed to touch!

Contents

Foreword

The following pages cannot tell you everything about model ship building — no single volume could do this properly. However, I hope this book will encourage you to make a start. The subject is infinitely interesting, full of history and with an end product of value that will give you much pleasure. The variety is endless and we have the whole of marine history to delve into with both easy ships to make and extremely difficult ones to tax the patience. There is the additional advantage that this is a relatively low-cost hobby.

No single ship or particular craft is described from start to finish. Structural detailing is of a general nature with references to the various periods and styles that give these wonderful old ships their date and place in history. Most model-making plans lack important detailing and many of the plans will be reproductions of real ship drafts. For instance, they will not tell you the kind of winch or anchor to make for that particular period or where the water barrel stood on the deck. This book will give you these details and help you to produce a model ship with real authenticity.

The tools you will need are few. The patience you will need is infinite! The results can be spectacular.

Introduction

Scratch built − what does this rather uninformative term mean? It means just that — from scratch. No carefully pre-manufactured parts, detailed instructions or packets of expensive pieces etc. In short, not a kit (as good as some of these can be for the real beginner).

This modest collection of information and drawings is intended as a continuing aid to all those model makers who want to try their hand at model ships. The model maker who wants more than the advertised list of old and famous ships available in simple kit form.

You will be making everything from dead-eyes to anchors. No, don't give up yet — it is not as difficult as you may think. Keep this book near your work bench as a reference. You will need a plan of course, then glue, nails, scrap wood, sandpaper and a few simple tools. A really superb model ship will cost you between £10−£20 made this way. A modest kit could cost £80 or more.

As final advice to all aspiring model ship builders of historic craft, try reading C. S. Forester, Alexander Kent and Dudley Pope's naval adventures. Apart from the wonderful excitement, you will learn much of the old terminology and all about the deck furniture and equipment. I would also recommend a trip to Portsmouth to see at first hand HMS *Victory*, HMS *Warrior* and the wonderful Naval Museum will put you into the right frame of mind for starting model ship building from scratch.

MODEL SHIPS
from scratch

Finding a plan

One of the simplest ways of procuring plans is to contact the staff of *Model Boats* magazine. They have a good plans service and are very helpful (see Appendix 1). On application they will supply a catalogue of various ship plans. Some of the advertisers in this magazine also run a plan service.

If you like researching the history of known ships there are many different books on the subject. However, as they usually contain many plans they are quite expensive so libraries and reference establishments are a good source for those with limited funds (see Bibliography). The National Maritime Museum is the custodian of many British and ex-American ship drafts.

Understanding ship plans

There are three basic points of information you will need to enable you to make the hull (body) of your model:
A. *Hull plan (body plan)*: this is a series of vertical cross sections taken through the width of the hull at even intervals (like slicing a loaf). On most plans these are numbered to avoid confusion. Section numbering starts at the stern (back end) to midships and is usually on the left of the plan. Numbering then continues from midships to bow (front end) and is on the right (see Fig. 1).
B. *Sheer plan*: this is the side elevation of the hull and the body plan verticals are drawn and numbered along this side view plan (see Fig. 2).
C. *Breadth (beam)*: this is a bird's eye view looking down on the profile of the hull. It shows the interval spacing of the body plan measurements. Also shown are the buttock lines, deck and water lines (see Fig. 3).

Fig. 1. Body plan.

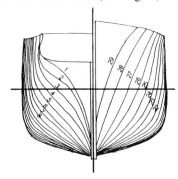

Fig. 2. Sheer plan.

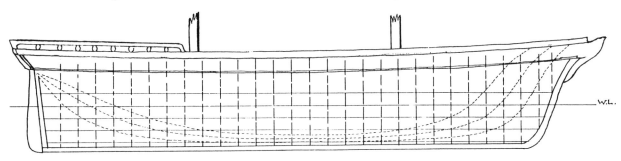

Fig. 3. Half breadth plan.

These are the bare essentials you will find on a set of plans. The best plans will show much more.

There are three main methods of producing a model hull in wood, (a) framed and planked form (see Fig. 4), (b) slab or sandwich form (see Fig. 5) and (c) solid carved form (see Fig. 6). We shall be concentrating on (a) and (c) throughout the following pages. There is a brief description of (b) for your interest.

The actual hull shape of the model you decide to make may dictate the type of construction followed. The further back we go in history, the fuller the hull designs become with acutely swelling bows necessitating high curvature at stem and stern. These curves are difficult to accomplish unless carved out of the solid as in method (c) above. When thinking about making a framed and planked form hull, try keeping to the hulls of the fast sailing ships from about 1780 onwards. These will be easier to plank and the method is similar to real ship building.

Notes on scale

The most popular scale is to ⅛″ which means one foot on a real ship becomes ⅛ of an inch on the model. This can also be defined as 1/96th size i.e. ⅛″ goes into one foot 96 times. For the more ambitious, ¼″ scale can be used but make sure your workshop or kitchen table is large enough!

Solid carved form hulls

Whether you are using a solid lump of timber or utilising a lamination of odd planks of the same wood to make your solid block, shaping it is hard but rewarding work as you see the shape emerging. This method is one of the quickest ways of finishing a hull ready for fitting out with all the interesting details. More about this on page 31.

Flat decked types are by far the easiest ships to start with such as some British fishing boats, Baltimore privateer schooners and most Royal Navy cutters of the 1770s.

If you decide on the more elaborate frigates from the eighteenth or nineteenth century with forecastle and poop decks, these raised portions can be made separately from the main hull and joined to it as illustrated (see Fig. 9a). Slightly raised decks fore and aft, like some fishing schooners, can be cut into the main hull shape while carving your hull (see Fig. 9b).

Slab or sandwich form hulls

Six layers of wood, each profiled as per plan, with their interior areas removed (see Figs. 7 & 8). The layers are glued together after careful positioning onto one another (see Fig. 8). This will be shown on plans for this type of construction. Exterior steps are planed away and finished following the plan profile. Interior steps can be

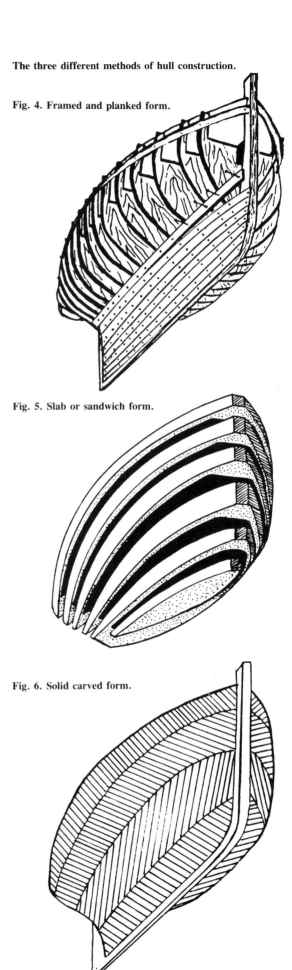

The three different methods of hull construction.

Fig. 4. Framed and planked form.

Fig. 5. Slab or sandwich form.

Fig. 6. Solid carved form.

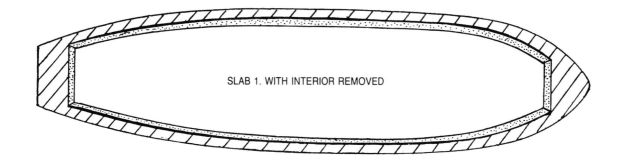

SLAB 1. WITH INTERIOR REMOVED

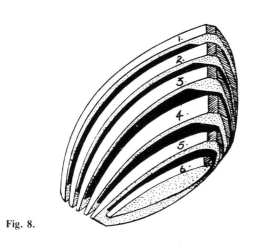

Fig. 7. Cross section after gluing together ready for removing exterior steps.

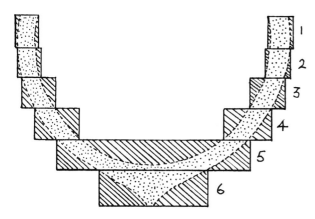

Fig. 8.

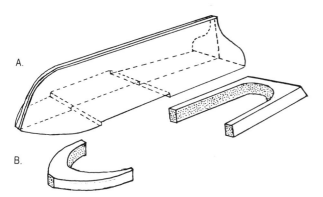

A.

B.

Fig. 9a & 9b. Solid form hulls.

left as in a fully decked model, these would not show of course.

This type of hull is favoured if the model maker chooses to sail the ship. It is fairly robust and leak-proof if waterproof glues and good paints are used and it is easier to make than the planked system of construction.

Framed and planked form

This type of construction is one of the best ways of making a hull. It takes longer to complete and lengthier descriptions are necessary, but the results are most rewarding as the model maker begins to feel like a real shipwright.

If you have a set of plans that are not to the size of your requirements, a method of reduction or enlargement has to be followed — this will apply for any type of construction you choose. The old-fashioned pantograph can be used and will give you a fair range of scales to work with. Enlarging or reducing by modern Xerox print machinery is another option. This method is the one I favour but try to avoid too great a jump in size or reduction from the original (your local print shop will advise you). Do not forget the scale you are working to.

With this type of construction you have to have your wits about you right from the start. Setting up the different bulk-head frames onto the keel using the plan is critical. But first we have to cut them out and make the keel assembly.

Taking these measurements off the plan is done by tracing. Some model makers favour the use of carbon paper, tracing through the plan onto a separate piece of paper. Whichever system you use, the tracing or the carbon impression is stuck onto the sheet of plywood in the case of bulkhead frames. Three-ply birch is probably the best material for this. The frames of many ship models I have made come from old junk drawer bottoms made of ply (⅛″ thick).

In the longer type of hull where there are no curves to worry about along the midship sections, it is worth considering the use of one or two ¼″ thick frames. The extra width is very helpful where planking joints can fall over this ¼″ thickness giving the butt ends of both planks something to bear on and plenty of room for pinning or nailing down without splitting the frames.

The Royal Navy cutter HMS *Fly* was one of 31 such craft bought by the Navy in 1763. These cutters had fine waterlines but were very broad in proportion to their length. They were weatherly craft able to carry huge sail areas.

The deck detail.

HMS *Fly*: the finished model.

The keel, stem and sternpost

For the making of these parts you must refer to the sheer plans, the side elevation. Trace off these shapes onto your material — most model makers use solid wood for this. Beech, lime or obeche are suitable, but of course stem and sternpost have to be glued to the keel using PVA wood glue, clamping carefully until thoroughly dry. Cutting all three parts in one from plywood is an option but it is not so strong and is inclined to bend on assembly unless fairly thick (see Fig. 10). Follow the plan for thicknesses here.

Before we use the keel, stem, sternpost assembly a groove has to be cut into each side of the stem post section to receive the ends of the planking eventually. This must follow the curve of planking on the stem (see Figs. 10a & 10b).

Deck support beam

This is the longitudinal deck beam in line with the keel and is cut from the same material as the keel assembly (see Fig. 10).

Bulwarks, gunwales and rail tops

It is worth mentioning at this stage of hull construction the various methods by which we make the wall of the ship above deck level. The bulwark is the planking or woodwork along the side of the ship above the deck that prevents the sea from washing over the gunwales — a term meaning the whole wall structure topped off with a stout rail.

The vertical woodwork that rises from deck level

17

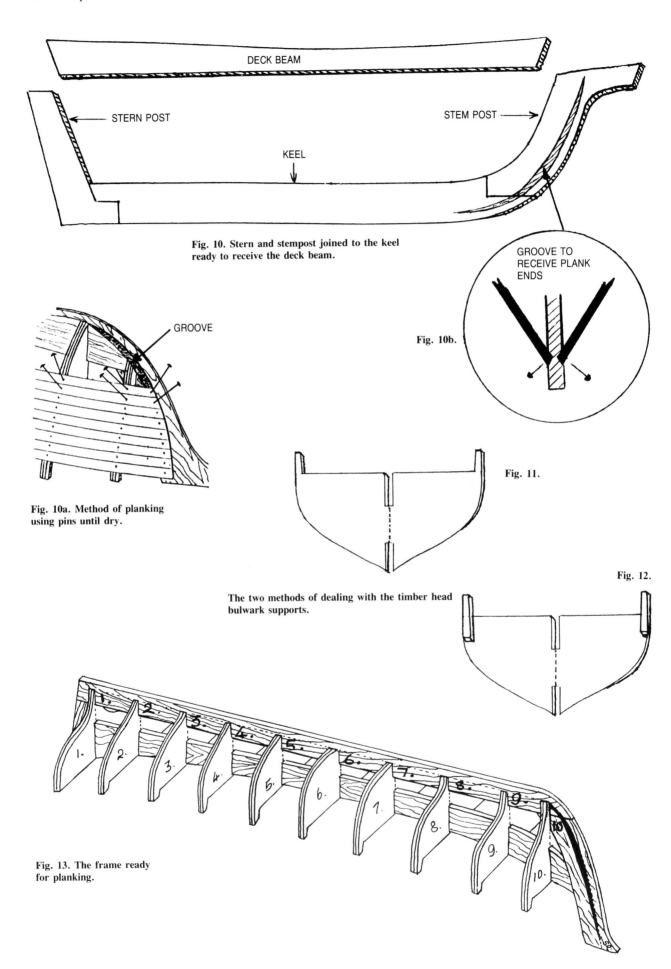

Fig. 10. Stern and stempost joined to the keel ready to receive the deck beam.

DECK BEAM

STERN POST

STEM POST

KEEL

GROOVE TO RECEIVE PLANK ENDS

Fig. 10b.

GROOVE

Fig. 10a. Method of planking using pins until dry.

Fig. 11.

Fig. 12.

The two methods of dealing with the timber head bulwark supports.

Fig. 13. The frame ready for planking.

(timber heads) to afford the fixings for the bulwarks can be an extension of the bulkhead frames or it can be glued separately onto the bulkheads before laying the deck planking. Obviously in the former method this extension, which is part of the bulkhead, will have to be cut in with whole piece (see Fig. 11). The other method of gluing these rising posts on to the bulkhead is stronger, providing you allow enough below deck level (see Fig. 12).

Bulkhead frames

When tracing these shapes off the body plan the centre line is drawn and then one side of the shape. By folding carefully down the centre line you can trace through for the other side, numbering each one as you do it. Don't forget to mark the deck level. When you have traced all the bulkhead frames, cut around the tracings leaving about 2 millimetres spare. Arrange the bulkhead tracings onto your plywood and stick down firmly into place with PVA wood glue. Now take your keel, stem and stern-post assembly and mark off carefully the different positions for the bulkhead frames to be attached, numbering each one carefully in the correct order from the plan information.

Taking the uncut sheet of bulkheads, draw in the slots for the keel and the deck support making sure that the centre line through the bulkheads, top to bottom, is central to the slots. Use dividers on all measurements.

Before cutting out the bulkhead frames re-check these slot measurements against the keel thickness as you are now at a point where the eventual shape of the boat and the deck level can go horribly wrong.

Cutting out is simple if you are lucky enough to have a fine cutting bandsaw or motorized fret-saw machine, but an ordinary hand fret-saw is very adequate. Whichever method you use, be very accurate. Always cut to the outside of the line and keep to this rule with every one of the bulkheads. Always cut the same way for the slots.

Rough assembly of the hull framework

You can try the fit of bulkheads to the keel assembly and the deck beam, making adjustments as necessary. Check that the bulkhead numbers correspond with those on the keel (see Fig. 13).

At this stage of construction all your careful work will start to look like a ship. If you are quite happy with the fit of all the parts you can now glue them together, checking very carefully the alignment of all the frames, making sure that keel and deck beam are at exact right angles to each and every frame.

When this assembly is dry the mast slots can be cut into the deck beams. Look carefully at side elevation sail and rigging plans for the correct angle of mast to deck (see Fig. 14 — a sheer plan of a Baltimore schooner). On some occasions I have forgotten to do this before laying the deck and have had to drill the mast holes through the deck and into the deck beams. This is not the best way!

If you intend stepping the mast butt onto the keel, as in a real ship, extra support pieces will be needed between the frames where the mast is (see Fig. 15).

Fixing the planking

I have seldom found it necessary to pre-bend planks before fixing to the hull frames. A lot depends on the type of plank wood and size of hull.

Dry bending with the aid of an iron (i.e. soldering) of medium size, can be tried. Gentle rubbing of the plank in the area you wish to bend while hand-bending the plank will help to set the curve. This method may be necessary with the acute curves at stem and stern of some models. Warm water applied on the exterior curve side can be tried. Before presenting planks to frames, the edge angle of each frame must be shaped — this is best accomplished by using one of the planks. Bend it

Fig. 14. Check correct angle of mast to deck when cutting slots in deck beam to receive masts.

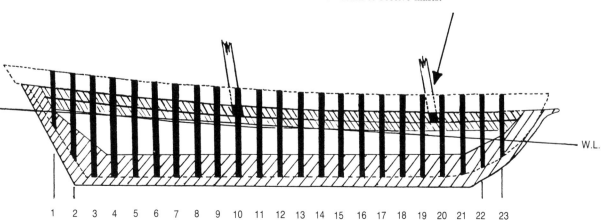

Fig. 15. Extra support pieces to be fitted if mast is to be fixed to keel.

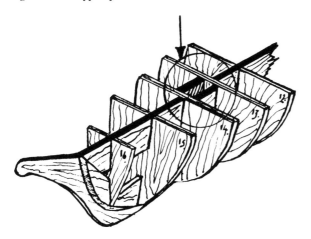

Fig. 16. Shave edges of bulkheads at bow and stern to receive planks at correct angle.

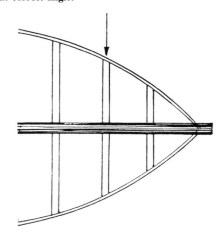

around the frame from stem to stern and note the angle. The wood must now be removed from the bulkhead frame edge to make a good fit of plank to frame (see Fig. 16).

Notes on planking material

There are no sacred rules about plank wood except that it should bend without too much cracking, be the correct thickness for the scale of the model and be readily available. Mahogany types, obeche, lime and some types of fine pine wood can all be used. I get most of mine from the scrap bins of a local furniture factory specialising in reproduction antique furniture of a high standard. The odd fiver in the tea box pays for this privilege. Maritime Models Greenwich will supply pre-cut planking very quickly by post together with their splendid catalogue of all things maritime (see Appendix 1 for their address).

If you are a practical type, and have any woodwork machinery like fine circular saws, you might try cutting your own planks from a solid baulk of timber.

The first planks are fixed at deck level on both sides of the hull. The deck may curve upwards slightly so this first set of planks may need bending upwards or even shaping a little to fit this deck sheer (upward curve).

Planks are attached with PVA wood glue. A dab of this on each frame edge and the plank is tacked with pins, knocked in with a small hammer or pressed in with pliers (see Fig. 10a). Pins should be left in place for at least half a day before pulling them out. Ordinary spring pegs and bulldog clips will also be most useful along the bulwark edge.

Continue planking on alternate sides. Lightly glue planks edge to edge as well as where they touch the frames. After three or four plank strips have been glued on both sides, any extra stern bulkhead or transom not already fixed to the keel can be carefully inserted (see Fig. 17, A).

Fig. 17. The stern bulkhead of some models cannot be fixed until a few planks are in place.

Some tapering of the planks that converge at the stern might be necessary, as in a counter stern ship. This will have to be done as each plank is presented to the frame before gluing. A similar operation may be necessary at the stem where planks are joined to stem post. This will depend on the swell of the prow area.

Again there are no hard and fast rules about planking except to warn about warping and twisting of the hull through misalignment and the unequal tension of planks on either side of the hull. The most crucial moment is when the first two planks (one on either side) are attached at deck level. Providing these are well glued and dry you could try to put on three or four planks, starting at keel level (see Fig. 4), although working from deck level to keel is the more common practice and is safer.

Keep sighting along the keel and deck beam as planking progresses so that stem, sternpost and bulkheads remain in perfect alignment. When planking is finished you could complete the bulwark above deck level or leave until the deck is laid.

Hull finishing

Using a selection of graded sandpapers, the hull is carefully rubbed down. You will notice that where the curves of the hull are acute, the edges of the planks will project slightly. Sand these edges off lightly. Depending on how accurate you have been, any faults can be attended to so do not be too depressed if your first attempts need a little attention.

Most hulls end up painted so cracks between planks can be filled with proprietary fillers and cleaned up with sandpaper. This, of course, is not ideal but as you progress with future models the need to attend to these slight discrepancies decreases.

Planking the deck

The laying of planks to the deck frames can be made in one of two ways. It is useful to remember that with 19th-century ships, planks were rarely wider than five or six inches, four to five inches being most common. Many of the deck planks were quite thick so these timbers in cross section were nearly square. Our model ship planks will not be to this kind of ratio. The lazy way to lay a model ship's deck is to use one sheet of thin model-maker's three-ply, scoring in the individual planks with a small spike and staining or inking-in the lines to give a planking effect. I recommend this method for very small models where the cutting of individual planks could prove difficult. Laying individual planks is by far the most satisfying way to proceed. Use the same material as used on the hull as long as the wood is not too dark. The plank widths should be in scale so do not make them too wide.

Start with the 'king' plank down the centre of the deck, working outwards towards the bulwarks. Apply glue to the tops of each frame as you work, not forgetting a little wipe of glue along each plank edge. Pin down each plank to every bulkhead it covers as you did with the hull planking. As this proceeds you will have to start angling the ends of each plank as they touch the bow and stern curves and eventually cutting slots to accommodate the bulwark posts that rise out of the deck edge (see Fig. 18).

Where the mast pierces the deck you will have to take careful measurements. Mark the plank with a small cross exactly where it will cover the mast hole in the deck beams, or work around the mast hole cutting planks to fit. Eventually we shall be making or simulating mast wedges at the foot of each mast.

In reality, deck planks were rarely in one piece for the whole deck length except in very small craft. In model making we can make fine knife cuts across the planks after they are well set to simulate plank butt joints (see Fig. 18).

There are occasions when a single sheet of thin plywood is laid down first onto the deck bulkheads before the planks are laid. If this is done, the extra deck thickness will have to be included in your calculations for bulwark height. This method is sometimes best for larger models, usually over two feet long. It helps with the stability of the hull and allows for the use of thinner planking on the decks.

In model naval ships of the 18th and 19th centuries, the bluff bows and highly curved stern sections make for some difficulties for the beginner. A lot depends on your skill and experience. If you can obtain a full-framed plan for one of these splendid naval ships and you feel confident enough to make a framed and planked vessel, it will need setting up in the same fashion as the real thing.

Solid sheet frames as previously described will not feature in these plans, but shaped timbers. These can be fret-sawed but you may like to consider miniature grown-shape timbers. This isn't as crazy as it sounds — try looking round your garden. Tree and bush trimmings of moderate sizes can be used when thoroughly dry. Fruit woods, bay wood, hawthorn, blackthorn and many other types can be used. Cut down their centre lengthways and squared up they make excellent frames, knees and crotches etc. Take a pair of stout clippers or a small saw with you on country walks and start a miniature timber yard.

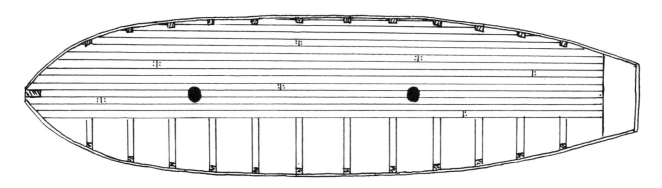

Fig. 18. Planking is cut to the bow and stern angle as it proceeds, where it touches the bulwark.

HMS *Mosquidobit* 1812 A Baltimore schooner. (© Edward Reeves of Lewes)

This charming ship is so American in its good looks and typifies some of the unique features found in small sailing ships of the period. She was originally built as a Letter of Marque ship. The British Navy captured her and changed her name from *Lynx* to *Mosquidobit*. This is a plank on frame model. The hull is left unpainted above the waterline. The wood is eggshell varnished. This kind of finish looks good providing your planking is nice and tight and correct, of course.

If you are set on making one of the old warships but are worried about the sharp curves you will encounter at stem and stern when making a planked hull, there is a composite way around this problem. Consider making the first bow and stern sections solid. Providing you allow for the thickness of the planking on the rest of the hull the joins will not show.

Solid carved form

There are several types of wood that we can use for hull construction — a soft Honduras mahogany is very good as are some types of straight grained pine, as long as there are no knots. A good cedar is fine although a little soft. In fact any type of wood that is not too hard and with a grain that is fairly straight and not too prominent. The 'Rolls-Royce' wood is lime but in block size the price is very high.

If you are lucky enough to find a single lump of any of the above timber, large enough for carving the whole hull from, then that will be ideal.

Another way to proceed is to find three or four flat planks of the same wood and glue them together using PVA wood glue, cramping them until dry. You can usually find plank off-cuts knocking around most work shops (see Fig. 6).

For the purpose of this exercise we shall assume that a frigate of the 1770s is to be made. This shaped hull demonstrates very well the reasons for choosing the solid carved form of construction for the beginner. The acute curvature at stern and especially at the stem are better coped with by carving rather than planking. However, you have a block of timber that has to be shaped. Before this happens you need to mark out the block with a centre line down its length, on the top and bottom side. Then from the breadth plan make a tracing of the breadth plan outline and centre line and transfer to the top and bottom side of the block of timber (see Fig. 19).

It is very important to note here that the breadth outline is taken at the main deck level. Frigates have a poop deck, (stern deck) and a forecastle deck (the deck at the bow). These two separate decks are higher than the main deck (see Fig. 21) and of reduced breadth as they curve towards their gunwale top (they 'tumble home'). See Fig. 22. The shaded part of Fig. 21 shows the area our block of timber constitutes at this stage. We shall be making the poop deck and the forecastle deck separately at a later stage.

The breadth-plan tracing can now be pricked through to the block or you can use the carbon paper method (see Fig. 19). The shaded portion of the illustration indicates the main area of wood that now has to be removed.

Cutting away the unwanted wood is done vertically through the block with a bandsaw or by the slower method of hand sawing, taking off small angled pieces and finishing with a chisel and plane.

You now have a boat-shaped billet of wood, flat at top and bottom, ready for carving. Before you start, mark

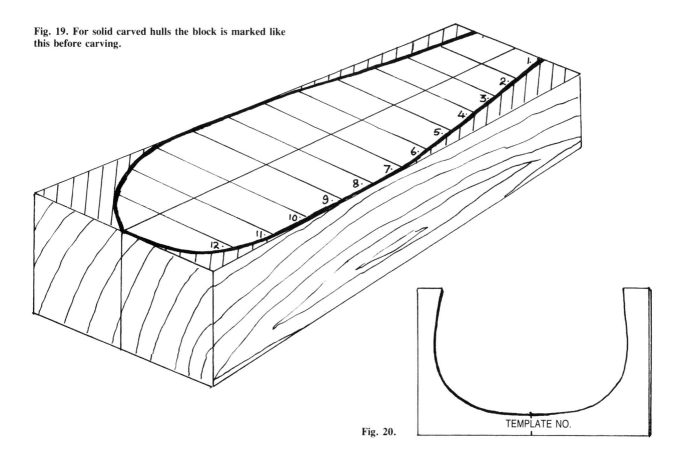

Fig. 19. For solid carved hulls the block is marked like this before carving.

Fig. 20.

TEMPLATE NO.

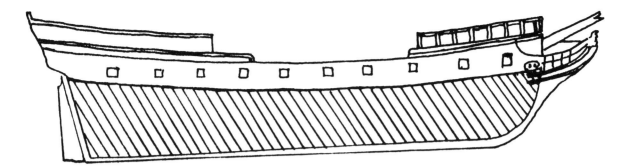

Fig. 21. The shaded area is how the block will look when carving is complete.

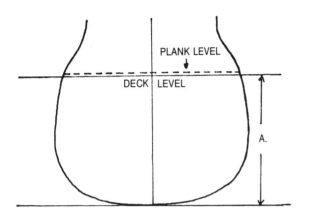

Fig. 22. You will be carving the area below the dotted line.

off across the block the different sections or stations taken from the breadth plan. These must be numbered (see Fig. 19). Now refer to the body plan. This also shows the various numbered cross sections vertically through the hull. Trace all these off onto stiff card, numbering each carefully. Again you must remember that these body plan cross sections of the hull must be taken from main deck level downwards to keel (see Fig. 22, A). Allow for deck plank thickness if separate planks are to be laid later. Cut out each shape carefully to make extra external templates of each cross section.

You can now start the carving process. The first stages can be made using a medium size plane. If you know how to use a draw knife then use this first. Place the block into a vice or work with the block, deck down, on a bench with a bench stop to prevent movement while planing. Keep the planing away from the centre line and concentrate around the edges. Keep your centre section templates at hand to check the hull curvature at the widest point as you proceed with the planing and carving process. You may feel happier using a sharp chisel or gouge and mallet for removing the wood. Remove wood slowly and in small amounts — you cannot put it back! You may find it useful to fix a vice-hold along the keel. A piece of stout dowel, like a broomstick section, can be screwed along the keel line. Place the dowel into the vice. This is useful while shaping, with the deck upwards

(see Fig. 23). This hold can be removed later. The slope of the stern can be cut at the correct angle as carving proceeds following the plan. The curve of the stem can also be shaped following the plan profile. Replace the centre guide lines at stem and stern — these will have been cut away during shaping.

The use of a sanding drum is something you may like to consider as carving proceeds. These spongy drums are easily fitted to most electric hand drills. You will need it bench mounted. The sanding bands for the drums come in different grades so choose the finer grades. I find the best way is to hold the hull firmly and present it to the revolving drum gently, keeping the hull on the move with a rolling motion. You will learn the kind of pressure to exert on the drum. Proceed with some caution using this method. It can be a very useful way of smoothing off carving marks but do not overdo it! These abrasive bands can remove unwanted wood at quite a rate. This is useful when carving the concave curve of clippers' prows providing the drum is of the right diameter.

As the rough carving reaches completion make sure you keep clear of the centre line drawn on stem, stern and keel. Be sure these are kept as flats. The best way to make sure of this is to draw parallel lines ⅛" away on either side of the centre line. Do not carve over these, only up to them.

You will, of course, use the templates throughout shaping the hull. As the templates for a frigate 'tumble home', i.e. swell to a maximum and then start to curve in a little, you will have to thread these on from the stern end each time you test the shape unless you cut them in half vertically to make a half template. Make sure each numbered template coincides with the numbered cross section lines on the hull drawn on the deck.

Before you start cutting the sheer of the deck which will remove your valuable markings, you must mark the sides of the hull, taking the line down about ½", at each station cross section so that you can redraw these lines across the deck after carving away for the sheer. The centre line will also have to be redrawn.

The sheer of the main deck, i.e. the curve, now has to be cut. Draw this curve onto the side of the hull each side. The maximum depth of this line will be in the

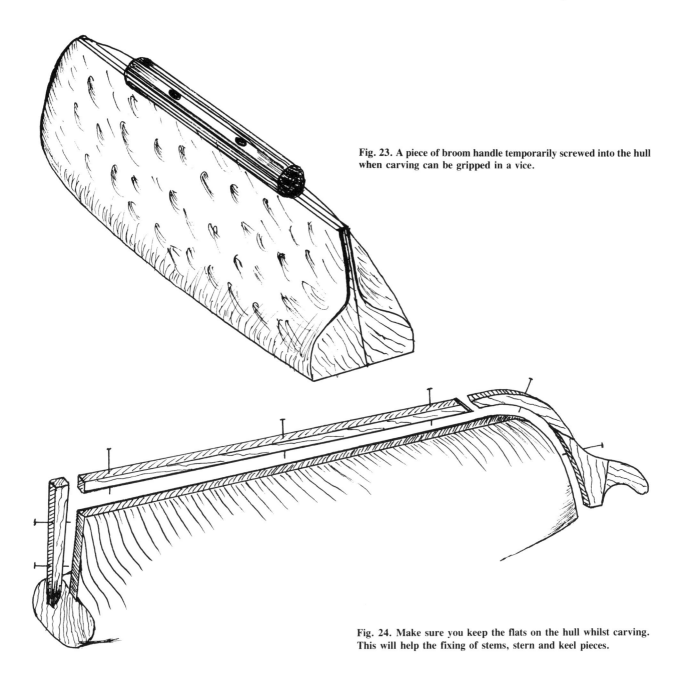

Fig. 23. A piece of broom handle temporarily screwed into the hull when carving can be gripped in a vice.

Fig. 24. Make sure you keep the flats on the hull whilst carving. This will help the fixing of stems, stern and keel pieces.

middle waist section of the deck. Remove this wood carefully with chisels and a small plane. You could use scrapers or a file to finish. Finally rub with sandpaper.

When you are satisfied that the hull is finally shaped to your satisfaction, test again with your templates or with calipers and the plan. Then finish off with sandpaper, coarse to fine.

Fixing keel, stem and sternpost

This is not difficult and is quite a relief after carving the hull. The keel and sternpost are in one piece each. The stem head is made up of three pieces shaped by fretsaw. They are glued and pinned onto the flats which were carefully left on the hull, the pins being withdrawn when

dry (see Fig. 24). In the real frigates of the period, the stern and stem head knees were made from grown curved timber where the grain would conform to the ship's curves. On model ships we can make these in pieces with simple angled butt joints from straight grained wood, no scarph jointing being required.

Building up the other decks and bulwarks

A frigate main deck had a complete sweep from bow to stern with no bulkheads to interfere with the movement of cannons on this main gun deck. For simplicity's sake we shall be making poop and forecastle decks solid, except for cutting them back a little under the deck top

25

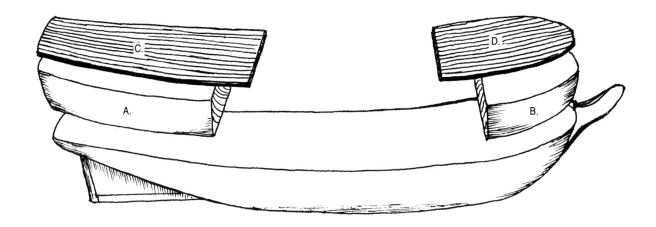

Fig. 25. The main hull carved and ready to receive the two blocks that will form the poop and forecastle areas.

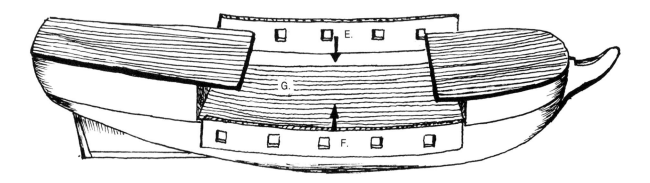

Fig. 26. The centre bulwark section is fitted when ready. Gun ports are cut afterwards.

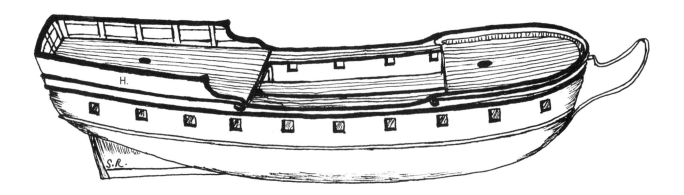

Fig. 27. The finished hull ready for fitting out.

to make it appear as if the main deck carries on under poop and forecastle (see Fig. 25). The experienced purist may choose a different method.

Examine your plans carefully and identify the length of both poop and forecastle decks. For their width, go by the width of the carved hull at bow and stern. The final width of these two decks at planking level will be narrower after carving. Choose two blocks of wood of the correct depth. Remember to reduce the length. As mentioned previously, we want to make it look hollow under the deck tops (see Fig. 25, A and B).

Having decided on the reduced length of these blocks place them on the hull in the correct position and draw around both using the main hull profile as your guide. Cut these out as you did the main hull following the line you have drawn. Tidy them up, checking that they are flush to the main deck outline when in position.

Poop and forecastle decks slope a little. When they are stuck to the main deck they follow the curve already carved on the main deck. Check the sheer plan and adjust if necessary.

We now have two options. Glue them to the main deck before carving or carve them roughly to the body plan profile before gluing down. If you have the patience, cut some more card templates for the area of the two decks from the body plan sections as before. If you have a good eye, calipers and a small ruler may suffice when carving.

Decking on this type of ship is easier if you cut the areas from the thin model-maker's plywood, scoring in the planking. Sheet decks can be stuck down before you fill in the waist bulwarks or left until after you do this (see Fig. 26, E & F). Measure and lay down the waist decking (see Fig. 26, G).

The bulwark should be measured-out making sure that the correct thickness of ply is used with the grain across the shortest side to facilitate bending (see Fig. 28). Over-cut the length of these so that you can force them gently between poop and forecastle deck causing them to bow a little. This will allow the bulwark to follow the hull curve. Also pay attention to the bottom edge of the bulwark where it joins the main deck. Not only does it curve very slightly (see Fig. 28, A) but an angle has to be shaved off this edge because it leans inwards slightly. Trial and error is the way here (see Fig. 28, B & Fig. 29, B). Try this before you cut the gunports and fix permanently. You can of course make these parts from solid strip wood and carve the necessary curves but ply is better for the beginner. You will need a little filler in the vertical joins, rubbed off with sandpaper. If you have shaped the poop and forecastle correctly the waist bulwarks where they join should be at the correct angle for the 'tumble home' effect. Entry ports are cut into the bulwark when the hull is ready to fit out. Having finished the carved hull, take a good look at it together with your plan. A shave here and there with a small plane or scraper and a little sanding may be necessary. Avoid making any flats in the curved areas caused by the tooling.

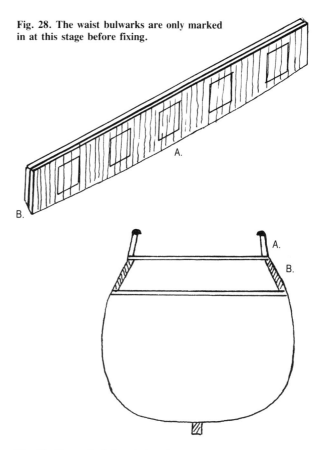

Fig. 28. The waist bulwarks are only marked in at this stage before fixing.

Fig. 29. The main bulwark B and the poop deck bulwark A.

Wales and strakes

You may come across these items of detail in a good set of plans for ships of the 17th, 18th and 19th centuries. These were thickened planks running round the hull which stood proud of the other planking forming a pronounced ledge. The main wale was at the waterline, or just above it, in ships of the late 18th century to the middle of the 19th century. The larger naval vessels from about the 1730s to the 1820s had a fairly wide band mainwale with two or three other narrower ones above, up to the deck level bulwark. These lengths of timber which formed the wale strakes could be built up from two to five plank thicknesses. The main purpose of wales, apart from strengthening the hull, was for protection when running alongside other vessels in battle. They also protected the gunport lids and other protruberances.

In reality most hulls started at the keel with fairly thick main planking. The planking reduced in thickness from the curve of the hull and thinned off towards the bulwark level. As hull designs improved from about the 1840s the use of heavy wales disappeared. By the 1860s the only thing left was a heavy rubbing strake on the outside of the hull below main deck level at the hull's maximum breadth. This protected the channel boards and hull planking when alongside other vessels or moorings.

Scott Robertson making a frigate. (© Windham Hime, Powys)

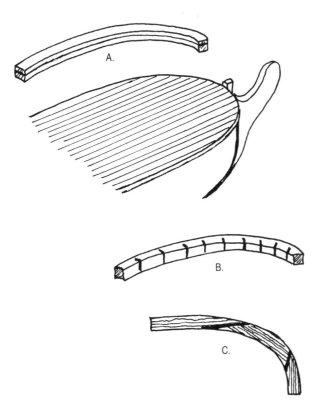

Fig. 30. Edging or margin boards can be made in one of three ways.

Much of the accentuated tumble-home shape of hulls disappeared after the 1850s.

Look carefully at your plan when fitting wales to the hull — they do not always follow the sheer line or deck line, nor do they follow the line of the gunports at bow and stern. This makes life a little difficult for the beginner. If all the gunports are established on your hull the positioning of the wales is made a little easier. This fitting is made with your leftover deck planking wood. You will find it much easier if you cut a card template and try it first against the hull. On some hull contours the template will turn out not just a simple curve but a double curve (see Fig. 30, D, E & F). It is better to establish this curve on one piece of planking first after you are happy with the template. Cut another plank layer from the first. Apply the first shaped plank to the hull with glue and pins. Some of the pins will have to be bent over to hold this first wale strake in place. When dry apply another until you have the correct thickness for the wale. Sand off gently when finished.

In some places the wale might touch or partly cover the edges of the gunports at bow and especially the stern in two- or three-decked ships. Do not worry about this. When all wales are fitted and dry you can re-establish the gunports by carefully carving with knife and chisel before fitting the port lids. This problem rarely occurs in smaller ships like naval cutters and schooners.

When all shaping and sanding has been finished, attend to the making of the poop deck bulwarks. These can be built up with thin strip layers, plywood or from solid flat strips (see Fig. 27, H & Fig. 29, A). On some frigates there is no solid bulwark, just a spray board with vertical timber posts rising out of the deck edge and topped with a stout rail.

In these bluff-bowed frigates the edging or margin boards that follow the bow curve on the deck edge will have acute curves and it may be easier if made in pieces. If made in one strip, cuts along the inner edge may be sufficient for the bending (see Fig. 30, A, B &C). They can also be fretted out of sheet wood, building up in layers.

Final note

When cutting gunports into the solid poop and forecastle area of the hull use a small sharp chisel. You need not cut too deep as these will be blackened when finished and fitted with gunport flaps (see Fig. 74, F to H). Transverse deck curvature is something we have not bothered with yet but here is a description of a simple method that avoids carving the slight curve. You can carve this while shaping the hull but in some types of hull it might be easier to use the following method. On small models it is hardly worth putting in this detail as it is scarcely noticeable when small hulls are finished.

Using thin plywood or thin stiff card cut to the profile of the deck. You cut the area a fraction larger by the amount taken out by the slight curve. By using a thin

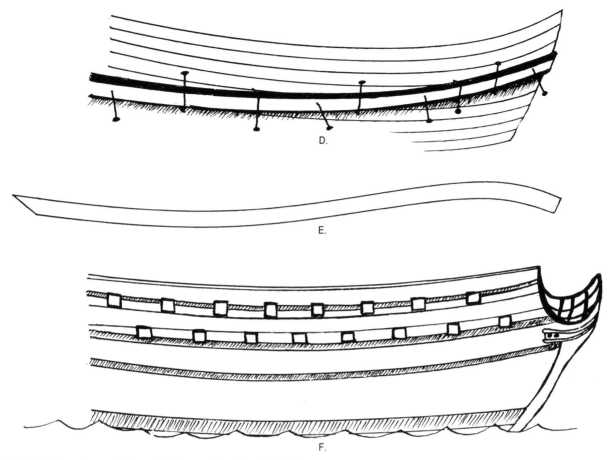

Fig. 30. The wales are thickened planks running along the hull and they do not always follow the sheer line of the deck.

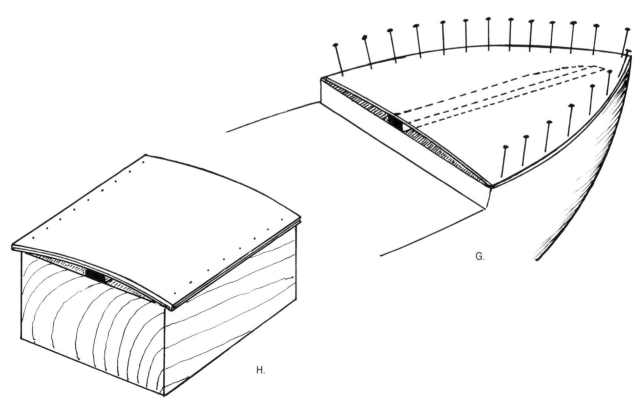

Fig. 30. Making curves in this fashion avoid carving them on the solid deck or hatch tops.

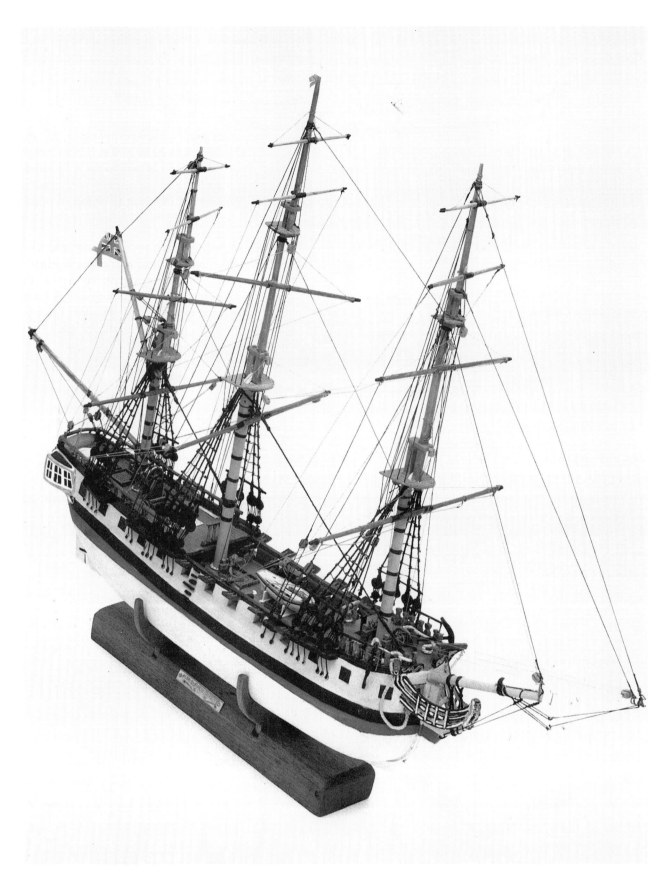

HMS *Raleigh* frigate 1776. (© Edward Reeves of Lewes)

The frigate *Raleigh* was a 32 gun ship made in Portsmouth, N.H. for the first American Navy in 1776. She was captured by the British in September 1778. In July 1779 she was put into dry-dock in Portsmouth, England, where her lines were taken off and a plan drawn. The Navy liked the design and wanted to make more like her but our ships proved to be heavier because of the large amounts of oak used. The Americans used much pine and pitch pine in their frigates, this made for a much faster vessel. The model in this picture is not quite finished.

strip of wood not more than $^1/_{16}''$ by $^1/_4''$ wide, stuck down along the centre of the deck, you cover this with the profiled deck sheet. Glue down the edges and pin until dry (see Fig. 30, G). This method of creating a curve can be used to great effect when a cabin roof or hatchway cover needs a curve, especially when the roof overhangs the structure a fraction. The space created by the curve can be filled in with your usual filler at each end and sanded off (see Fig. 30, H).

If you think that carving a hull from scratch is going to be difficult, do not let this put you off. Some model shops can supply rough carved hulls. Look at the advertisements in *Model Boats* magazine. This will get you going and you can always practise this part of the craft until you feel confident enough to start literally from scratch on the hull.

Fitting out

A general description of the two main methods used in hull construction has been given at some length. The fitting out of model ship hulls can now begin. As you will see from the list below, there is much to do.
1. Masts, yards, booms and gaffs.
2. Standing and running rigging.
3. Rudders, steering, deck gear and hatches.
4. Armaments.
5. Finishing and painting.
6. Sails.
7. Mounting stand.

The descriptions and drawings which follow will apply to the fitting out of both types of hull previously described and be relevant to many more types of craft.

Masts

Masts were rarely made as one section, except for small sailing craft. On larger ships they were made with two or three sections. The lower section of these tapered very little. Many were made from solid straight pine tree trunks. The shortage of this type of timber eventually resulted in the masts being made in four or more pieces; a central square core surrounded by four cheeks of timber and shaped into a round. Bolts and iron hoops spaced at regular intervals held everything together — this probably made for a stronger mast. The next section of mast was called the top mast, the third section, the top gallant mast (see Fig. 31). You will see from this diagram that there were eight separate sections of mast for ships that had a foremast, main and mizzen mast.

MAST KEY.

A.	Main topgallant mast	K.	Fore topmast yard
B.	Fore topgallant mast	L.	Mizzen crossjack yard
C.	Mizzen topmast	M.	Main mast yard
D.	Main topmast	N.	Foremast yard
E.	Fore topmast	O.	Mizzen gaff
F.	Mizzen mast	P.	Mizzen boom
G.	Main mast	S.	Main topgallant yard
H.	Main foremast	T.	Fore topgallant yard
I.	Mizzen topmast yard	Q.	Bowsprit
J.	Main topmast yard	R.	Jib boom

Fig. 31.

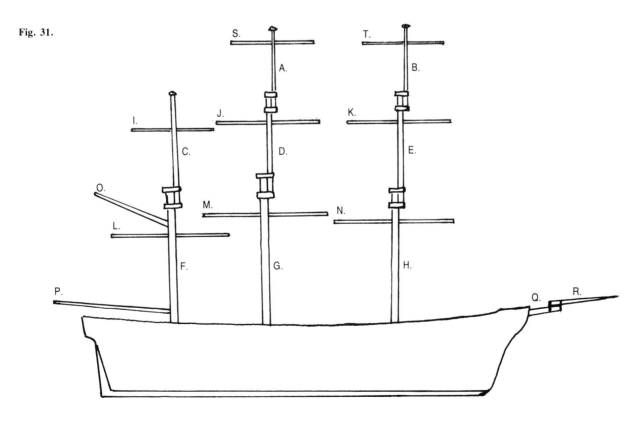

31

Fig. 32. Masts are never round throughout their length so watch the size of the timber you start with.

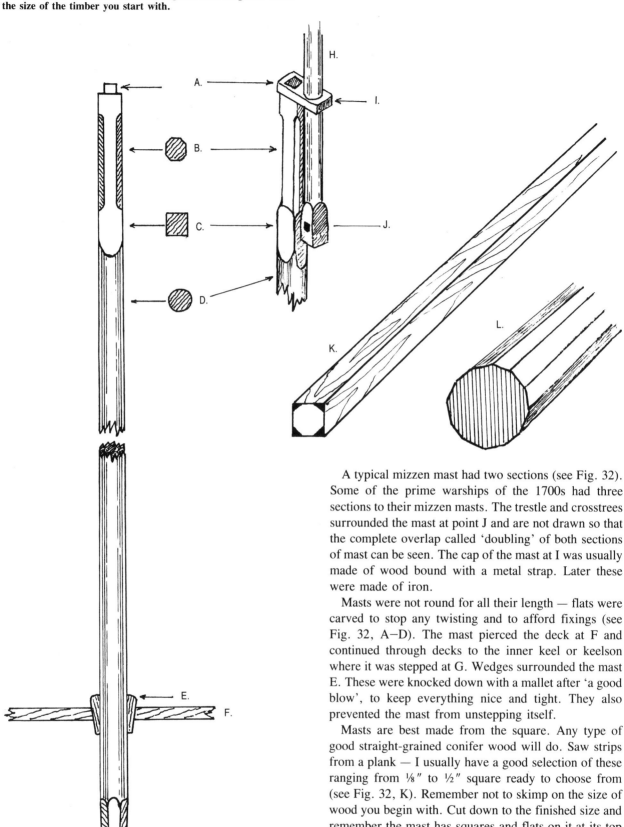

A typical mizzen mast had two sections (see Fig. 32). Some of the prime warships of the 1700s had three sections to their mizzen masts. The trestle and crosstrees surrounded the mast at point J and are not drawn so that the complete overlap called 'doubling' of both sections of mast can be seen. The cap of the mast at I was usually made of wood bound with a metal strap. Later these were made of iron.

Masts were not round for all their length — flats were carved to stop any twisting and to afford fixings (see Fig. 32, A–D). The mast pierced the deck at F and continued through decks to the inner keel or keelson where it was stepped at G. Wedges surrounded the mast E. These were knocked down with a mallet after 'a good blow', to keep everything nice and tight. They also prevented the mast from unstepping itself.

Masts are best made from the square. Any type of good straight-grained conifer wood will do. Saw strips from a plank — I usually have a good selection of these ranging from ⅛" to ½" square ready to choose from (see Fig. 32, K). Remember not to skimp on the size of wood you begin with. Cut down to the finished size and remember the mast has squares and flats on it at its top (see Fig. 32, B & C).

I find it best to make the whole mast with all the sections, crosstrees and detailing on the work bench, assembling it with the tops and then trying it on the hull. On very large models this may not be the best approach.

Tops and crosstrees

The terminology for the structure around the head of the lower mast is explained as follows (see Figs 33 & 34). The whole structure with its platform is called the top (see Fig. 35). This comprises crosstrees, A & B and trestletrees, C and D (see Fig. 33), these rest on the cheeks or bibs (see Fig. 34, G). This frame is boarded over to form a platform. The structure, if on the head of the top mast, is called the crosstrees and is rarely, if ever, boarded over.

To make the crosstrees see Fig. 33, L. You may find simpler ways than shown, remembering that the finished frame must be flat to receive the boarding over. The tops in an average sized model may measure only 1¾ " to 2" across. The boarding of the top can be made in one or two pieces using thin veneer or ply. Score on the boarding with a scribe. The pattern of boarding varies with the period (see Fig. 35) — this is a naval top of 1750 onwards. This is a good time to drill the shroud holes around the edge of the top (see Fig. 35, M).

You will see from Fig. 35, J that the boards are not over the whole top. The spaces left unboarded are for the lower mast shrouds which go over the bolster piece and around the main mast just above the platform.

Tops have many uses. They afford a fixing for the upper shrouds at their edges. This part of the standing

Figs 33–35. Tops and crosstrees.

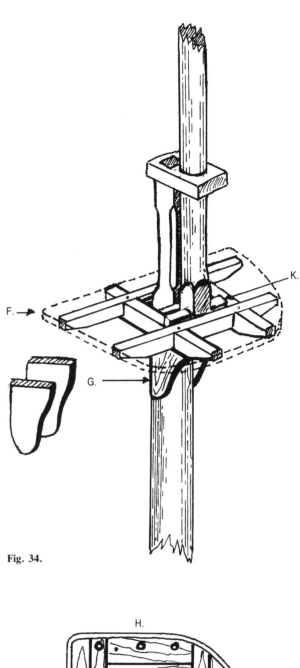

Fig. 34.

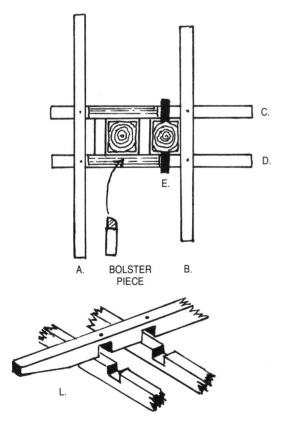

Fig. 33.

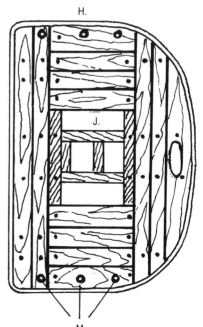

Fig. 35.

Mk I.

The British Trading Cutter *Gem* 1835

The pictures show (top to bottom print) the first and second attempts at the ship. As so often happens, the first turned out better than the second.

The colours were altered for both vessels, so was some of the deck furniture.

Mk II.

Mk I.

British trading cutter *Gem* built in 1835. She weighed 52 tons and was very similar in looks to the British naval cutter of the late 1700s. Carvel-built on the Isle of Wight, she ended up in Australian waters trading. Finally she perished not far from Fremantle in May 1876. This is another good type of model to start with. It only has a single mast and the rigging is reasonably simple.

Foredeck of Mk II.

The Catalan Boat. (© Edward Reeves of Lewes.)

This weird looking vessel, circa 1440, was made from plans taken off the original shipwright's model. In the early part of this century the original hung up in the Hermitage of San Simon de Mataro. It was stolen and turned up in an antique market in Munich in 1920. A wealthy Dutchman bought and presented it to the Prins Hendrik Museum in Rotterdam where it can still be seen. It is probably the earliest original European model of a sailing ship in existence.

The model I made entirely from sheet oak built up on solid frames of ply.

Copies of plans can be obtained from Borras Ediciones, Diputacion 296 Entio 1A, Barcelona 9, Spain. Price on application.

rigging gives lateral support to the top mast at an effective angle (see Fig. 37). They formed a frame around the two masts giving a purchase for a wedge, usually made of steel or lignum vitae, called a 'fid' that goes through a tapered hole at the butt end of the top mast (see Figs. 33, E & 34, K). When boarded over they are essential for the crew to use when rigging and sail setting and give a good platform for the 'look-out' and the musketeers!

Tops vary in design with the period. In the 15th century they were usually round and earlier these were the crows' nests. See photos (pages 36 & 37) of the Catalan ship 1450. In the 16th and 17th centuries they became larger tops, merchant and naval ships having different designs. The prime fighting ships of Nelson's time had fighting tops of twenty feet wide! In battle, marine marksmen would use them as musket platforms. Nelson is said to have died from a French musket ball fired from this position.

Modelling these parts is fun after all the hard work of the hull.

The finished model fitted with one mast only.

The model during construction.

Booms and gaffs

Booms and gaffs can be made from different diameters of dowling, better still from square-cut pieces that can be planed and scraped into shape, providing you choose straight-grained softwood (see Fig. 36).

Like masts they have to be shaped and tapered from the square. Go by the sail and rigging plan for their different lengths (see Fig. 36).

A little planing board is very useful and is made easily from a scrap piece of plank (see Fig. 36, G). Fix a small stop at the end of the V that should be low enough not to interfere with planing. If long enough you can use it with masts.

Booms and gaffs have jaws at their thick end. These act like a saddle against the mast allowing movement around it. To help this, and to prevent the jaws from jumping off the mast, a parral was used. This consisted of a rope threaded with trucks made of wood and ball

shaped. Parrals were fixed to each side of the jaws and helped the gaff up the mast when hoisting it and on the boom when bracing around the sail. You can use small beads threaded to cord for the parral (see Fig. 36, C).

Make the jaws by gluing two pieces either side of the boom or gaff, shaping with a file and sandpaper (see Fig. 36, A).

On some ships the gaff jaws were curved allowing the gaff to sit at a higher angle than the straight pattern (see Fig. 36, E).

The boom sat on a ledge around the lower mast called a boom jaw rest. These would circle the mast completely or be half rests (see Fig. 36, D).

Both gaffs and booms appear in ships on the mizzen mast (see Fig. 36, F), but on schooners they are on main and mizzen and any ship that sports fore and aft sails. Sometimes a ship would hoist a sail on the gaff pole only. The bottom of the sail is then said to be loose-footed (without boom).

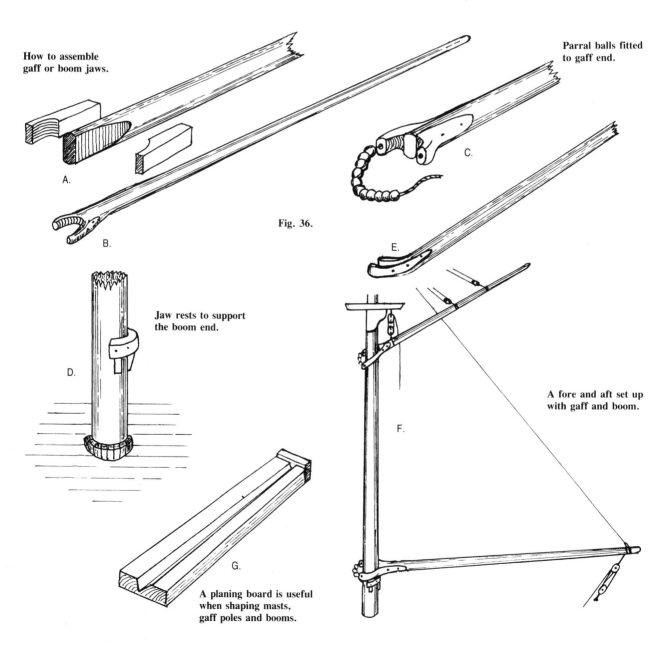

How to assemble gaff or boom jaws.

Parral balls fitted to gaff end.

A.

B.

C.

Fig. 36.

E.

D.

Jaw rests to support the boom end.

F.

A fore and aft set up with gaff and boom.

G.

A planing board is useful when shaping masts, gaff poles and booms.

Fittings on gaff and boom

Fittings varied from ship to ship. The boom supported the foot of the large fore and aft sails on the mizzen mast called a spanker. This needed stretching tight along the boom. Sails were usually lashed to the boom in a number of ways with a continuous rope (see Fig. 38, A).

Study Figs 38 & 39 and you will see that they show a lot of detail that is useful to understand, even if we do not include all of it in our model. We can cheat a little here and there. Fittings, and how to make them are described later.

Fig. 37.

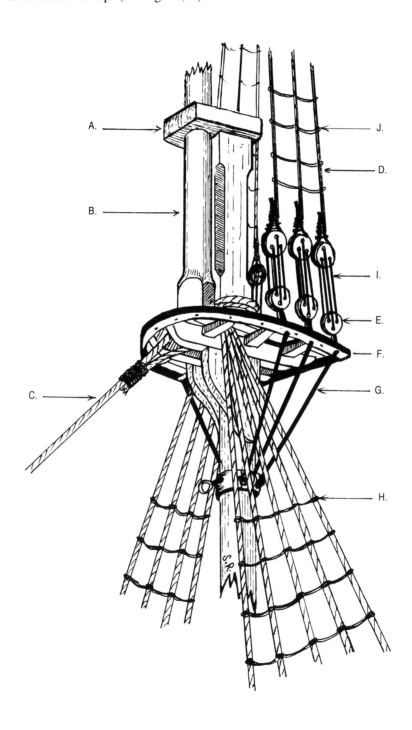

A TOP OF THE 1850s

A.	Lower mast cap	F.	The top
B.	Top mast	G.	Futtock shrouds or stays
C.	Main stay	H.	Lower mast shrouds
D.	Top mast shroud	I.	Lanyards
E.	Deadeyes	J.	Ratlines

Fig. 38.

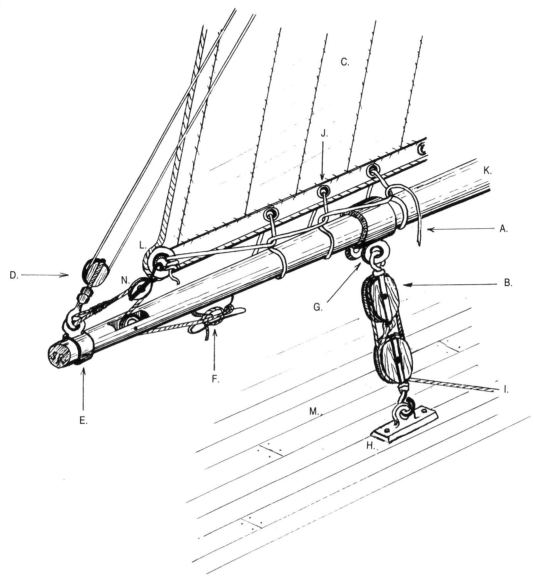

THE MIZZEN BOOM

A.	Foot lashing rope	H.	Ring plate, deck ring
B.	Main sheet blocks	I.	Main sheet
C.	Sail	J.	Lashing eyelets
D.	Topping lift block	K.	Boom
E.	End boom band	L.	Thimble cringle
F.	Boom cleat	M.	Deck
G.	Main boom band	N.	Clew block

Yards

Yards are not difficult to make — the shaping process is the same as for the masts, gaffs and booms. Yards were thick at the middle, tapering off towards their ends. A quarter of the total length was eight-sided at the centre, usually going into a round for the rest of the length. The bands would grip better on an eight-sided timber at the centre of the yard where it was joined to the mast (see Fig. 45, A & M).

Whatever period of model ship you are making it was the method of suspending the yards and the system of lowering them where changes took place, depending on the period. There are no hard and fast dates — the systems overlapped over a period of years.

Use small squared-up pieces as for other spars on the model ship. Be careful not to make the ends pointed — you will need room to drill each end to look like a

Fig. 39.

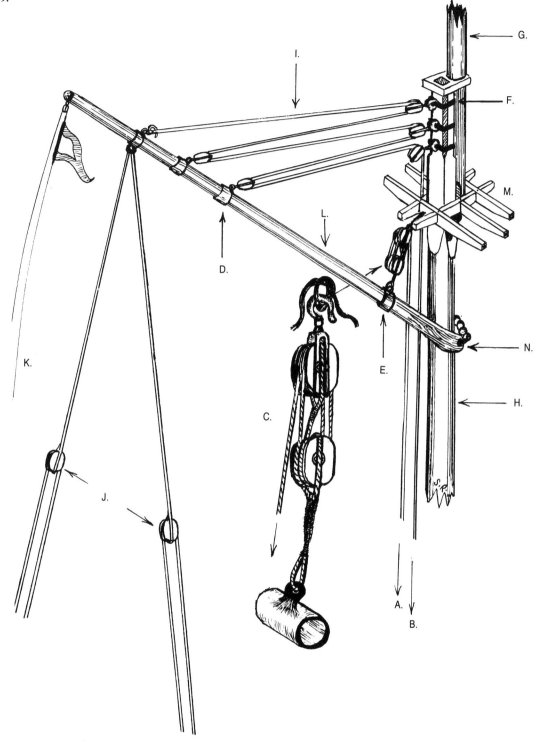

THE MIZZEN GAFF RIGGING

A. Throat halliard
B. Peak halliard
C. Double purchase tackle
D. Gaff halliard bands
E. Gaff halliard throat bands
F. Mast bands at doublings
G. Top mast

H. Lower mast
I. Peak halliard
J. Vang and blocks
K. Signal or flag halliard
L. Gaff
M. Crosstrees, unboarded
N. Jaws and parral

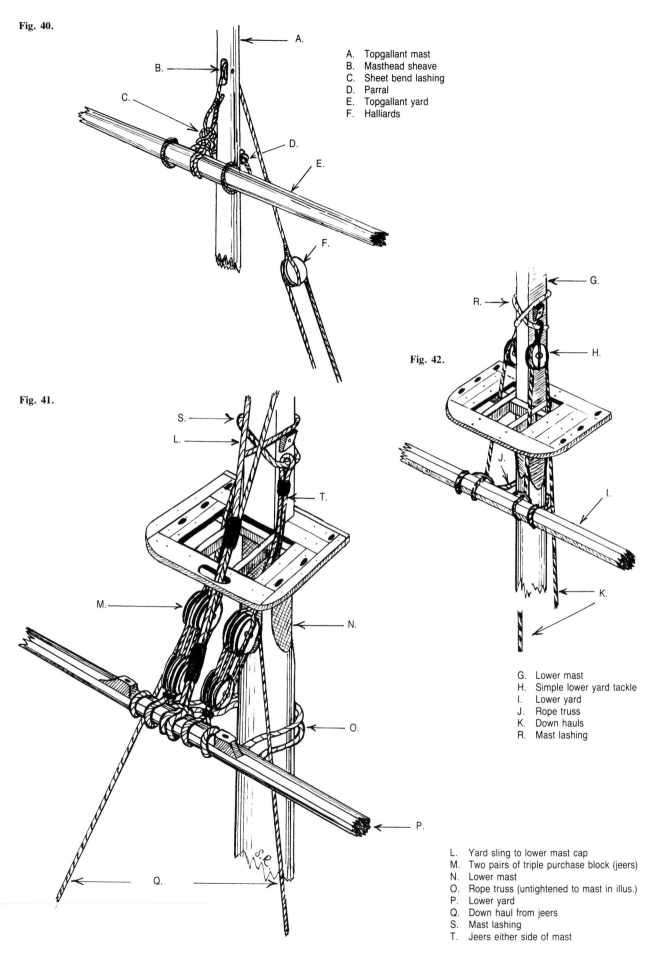

Fig. 40.

A. Topgallant mast
B. Masthead sheave
C. Sheet bend lashing
D. Parral
E. Topgallant yard
F. Halliards

Fig. 42.

Fig. 41.

G. Lower mast
H. Simple lower yard tackle
I. Lower yard
J. Rope truss
K. Down hauls
R. Mast lashing

L. Yard sling to lower mast cap
M. Two pairs of triple purchase block (jeers)
N. Lower mast
O. Rope truss (untightened to mast in illus.)
P. Lower yard
Q. Down haul from jeers
S. Mast lashing
T. Jeers either side of mast

sheave. Finish as on previous spars. Some were oiled and varnished, others were painted. More about this later.

Yards vary in design within the same ship. Depending at what point they are attached to the mast, the higher up the simpler the design becomes.

Starting at the lower mast is the lower yard (see Fig. 45, B & D). These were rarely if ever lowered, except when being replaced after damage in war or from weather. They were held in place by rope yard slings and a rope truss around the mast. In addition, the yard was supported by very large blocks and tackle, called jeers, a lowering device for use as mentioned earlier (see Fig. 41, M). This heavy tackle added additional strength

to a vulnerable area in battle and this system was used by naval ships up to the 1800s approximately.

Small ships had lighter tackle, again using a rope truss to keep the yard to the mast and just a pair of pulley blocks (see Fig. 42).

Moving up to the next section of mast, the top mast — here the top sail yard was attached. Naval ships had robust tackle (see Fig. 43). Up to the 1800s this yard was raised and lowered by halliards and rode on parrals around the mast. The heavy tackle required double tyes as fixed points either side of the mast just under the topmast cap. The other end of this rope became the halliard, after passing over a double and single block pulley (see Fig. 43, A).

Fig. 43.

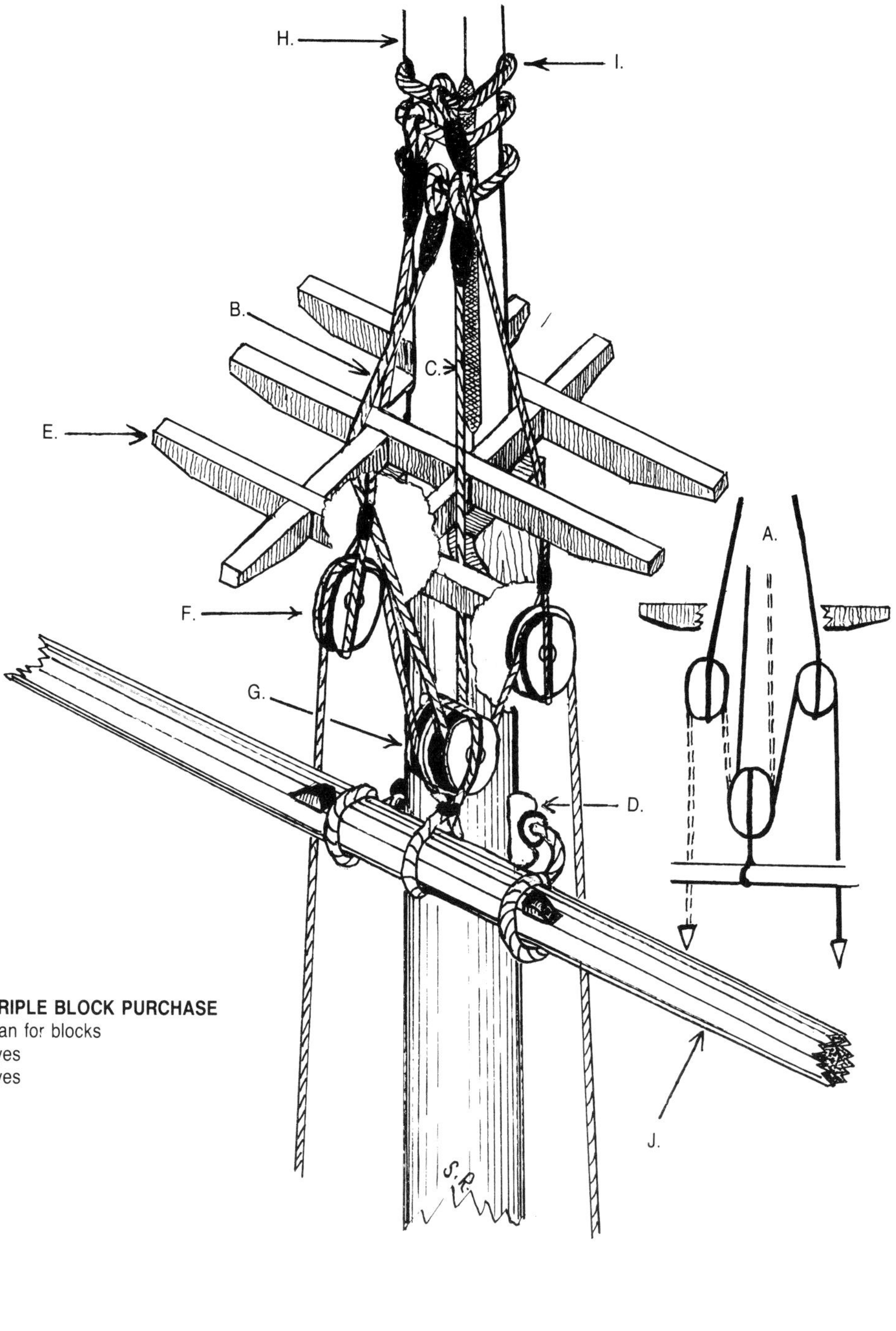

TRIPLE BLOCK PURCHASE
A. Rope threading plan for blocks
B. Standing end of tyes
C. Standing end of tyes
D. Parral
E. Crosstrees
F. Single block
G. Double block
H. Topmast
I. Mast lashings
J. Topsail yard

Fig. 45.

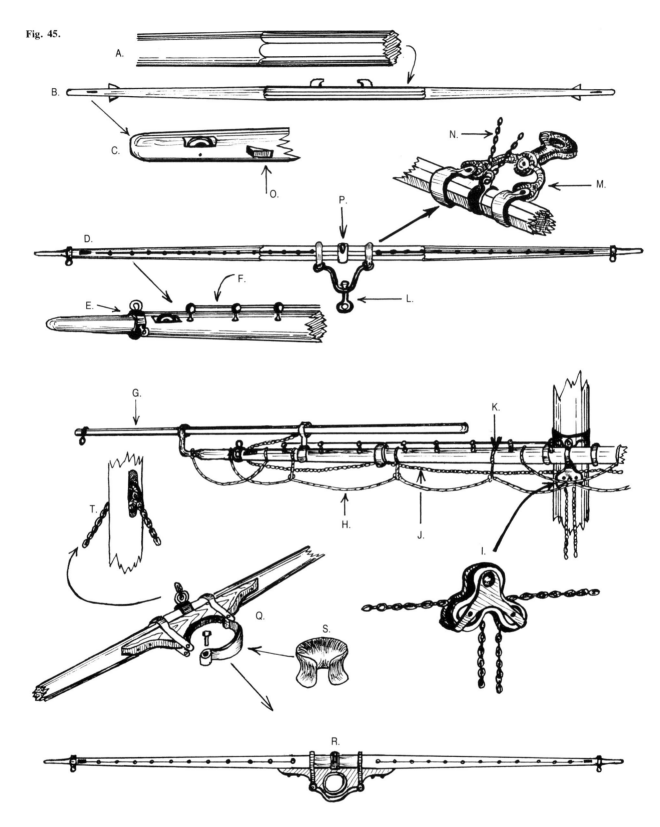

A.	Yard centre eight sided	K.	Stirrup rope to footrope
B.	Lower yard — before 1800s	L.	Iron swivel — 1850s
C.	Yard end — sheave and cleat	M.	Detail if iron trusee swivel 1850s
D.	Lower yard — before 1850s	N.	Chain sling to mast
E.	Yard end, band & sheave	O.	Wooden cleats for sail ring
F.	Jackstay bar	P.	Band for chain sling
G.	Studding sail boom	Q.	Yard yoke & tub parral
H.	Foot rope	R.	Topsail yard — 1850s
I.	Double sheet block	S.	Iron liner for tub parral
J.	Chain sheet to boom	T.	Chain sling to mast sheave at masthead

Note G, H, I, J & K show a 19th century yard.
Earlier types were less sophisticated.

Lighter tackle was used on smaller sailing ships, sometimes a rope truss to the mast or simple parral holding yard to mast.

Moving still further up the mast we come to the topgallant yard. The support here becomes lighter, the yard being suspended on a rope, sheet bended around the yard then through a sheave in the mast over a pulley (see Fig. 40). The tye and parral method held the yard to the mast.

Yards were also set on the mizzen mast to serve the square sails above the fore-and-aft set of sails. The first yard, called a cross-jack, formed the attachment for the clews (bottom corners) of the mizzen topsail. The term cross-jack applies to any fore-and-aft rigged ship which sets a yard below the lower crosstrees.

Having now described the four main types of yards used in the 1800s to 1850s, it will be useful to understand some of the improvements made during and after that period, namely the double topsail and the addition of jackstays (see Fig. 46).

Jackstays

These were introduced in the early 1800s. Sails before this were attached to the yard by a simple lacing robband passed through the sail eyelets and around the yard. The jackstay consisted of a series of eyebolts screwed to the top of the yards. A rope was then threaded along the top of the yard through each eyebolt and made tight and secure at the centre of the yard. This rope was eventually replaced by an iron rod. The sail could now be lashed to the rod from the individual sail eyelets, it then hung down over the front of the yard.

The double topsail

It was essential that topsails should be reefed or furled as quickly as possible when a squall or storm hit the ship. Most topsails were in one piece (see Fig. 47), but around the 1840s this sail area was divided in two (see Fig. 48). This made reefing much lighter work and quicker and therefore safer. An extra yard was now necessary, this being swivel-fitted to the lower mast cap.

A DOUBLE TOPSAIL AND ROYAL MAST 1850s
A. Royal yard
B. Topgallant yard
C. Upper topsail yard
D. Lower topsail yard
E. Lower yard
F. Iron cap and crane fitting
for lower topsail yard.

Sail Names
1. Royals
2. Topgallants
3. Upper topsails
4. Lower topsails
5. Main sail (or Main course)

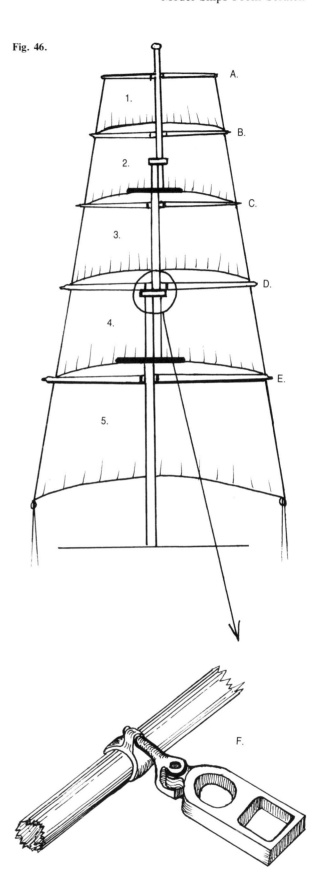

Fig. 46.

Note The mast illustration Fig. 46 is drawn sideways to show the different steps of mast although the sails are drawn correctly, as viewed frontwards.

Fig. 47.

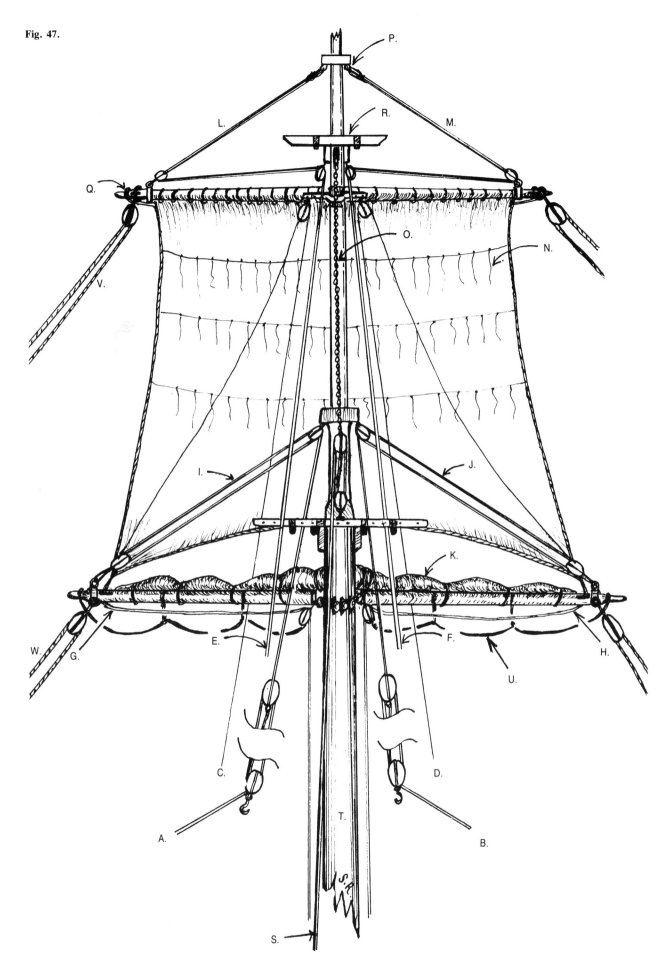

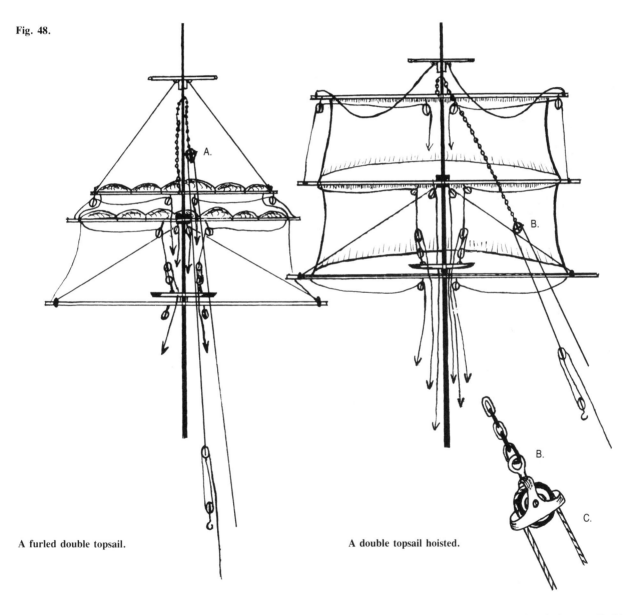

SINGLE TOPSAIL 18th & 19th CENTURY	
A.] Lower lift purchase hook	N. Reefing points
B. } to eyebolt on channels	O. Chain tye
C.] Clew lines to lift sail	P.] Standing rope lift attachment to
D. } for furling	} top mast
E.]	Q. Sail ring
F. } Top sail yard lift	R. Top mast crosstrees
G.] Top sail sheet	S.] Halliard from chain tye purchase to
H. } Clew lines	} heavy cleat or kevel at deck
I.] Lower yard lift	T. Lower mast
J. } Ropes	U. Foot ropes
K. Furled main sail (main course)	V.]
L. } Standing ropes top	W. } Braces (naval ships)
M.] yard lift	

Fig. 48.

A furled double topsail.

A double topsail hoisted.

The cap was now made of iron, and the fore-end moulded to receive a crane fitting to the yard (see Fig. 46, F).

The upper topsail yard was lifted and lowered by a chain tye attached to the upper topsail yard. The other end of the chain tye was attached to an iron gin block (see Fig. 48, A, B & C). The topmast was pierced and

sheaved with a pulley over which the chain travelled just under the topmast crosstrees. The gin block pulley carried the ropes that terminated as topsail halliards, one end to a purchase at the deck level waterways (i.e. the outside planks of the deck), the other end hooked in the opposite waterway (Fig. 48, B shows both going to one side but be guided by the description).

The brigantine *Leon* circa 1880

This model was built from a set of old plans by that well known expert Harold A. Underhill, MC, AMIES. Plans by Mr. Underhill are some of the best if you can obtain them. The original ship was built in Laurvig, Norway.

Fig. 49. Three different types of bulwarks.

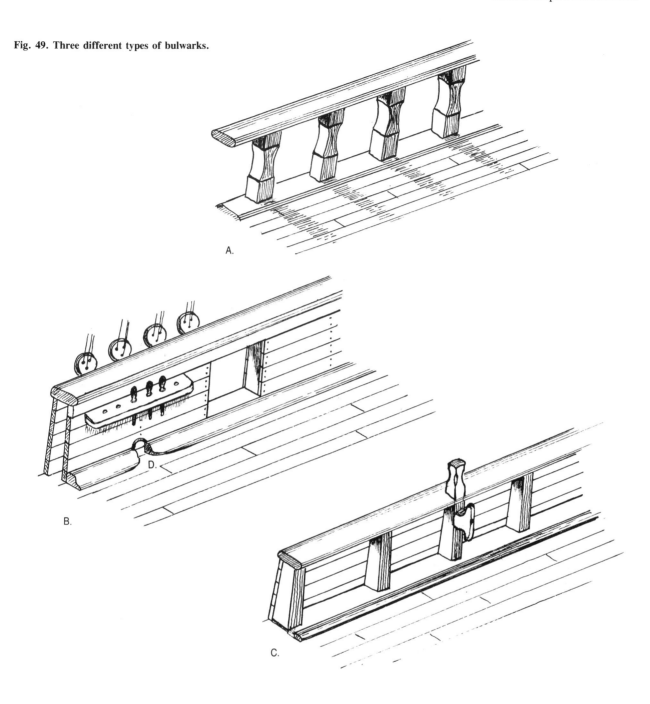

A.

B.

D.

C.

Bulwarks

In the illustration you will see three different types of bulwark (see Fig. 49, A, B & C). In A the timberheads (i.e. the frame timbers that continue above deck level, sometimes only the alternate ones) are left unplanked and carved. In B planking is on the outside and inside, as in warships needing the extra strength. (See the gun port and belaying pin rail.) D is a scupper hole to drain deck water. In C is a typical merchant ship bulwark, planked on the outside of the timberheads only. One of these is extended above bulwark level and shaped, making a vertical kevel head. Also bolted to this is a cleat. See the illustration comparing two different poop decks and their respective bulwarks (Fig. 50, F & G). In F the deck is only partly raised, the bulwark is planked on one side only. This is a fishing schooner of about 1880. In G we have a much higher poop deck with panelled front, a merchant ship of the 1880s.

Kevels

These were heavy-duty belaying points along the inside of the bulwark, usually very robust (see Fig. 50, A—E). In D this kevel was used on the forecastle deck and took the end of the catting tackle (hanging the anchor) from the cathead sheaves. In E this vertical kevel with sheave took the lower yard lift rope or topsail halliards. All these were types used up to about the 1800s.

Making them for our model is simple — be guided by the illustrations and try to keep edges sharp.

Fig. 50.

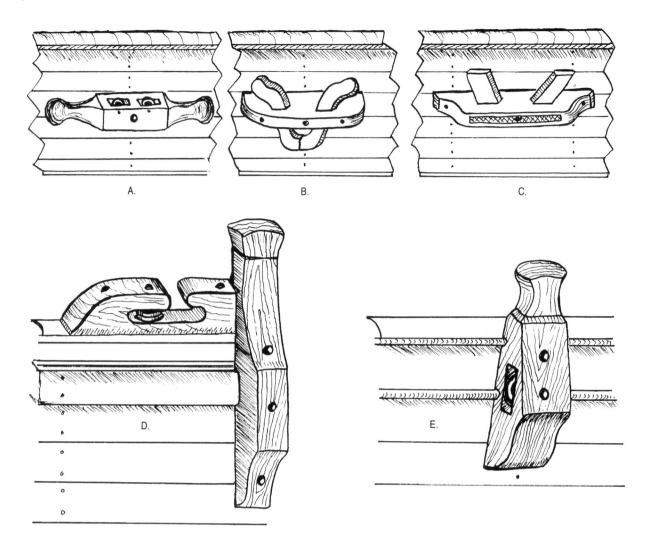

A.   B.   C.

D.   E.

Various types of kevels or belaying points.

F.   G.

A fishing schooner poop deck 1880.   A merchant ship's poop deck 1880.

Although this book concentrates on building ships from scratch, a lot of fun can be had from rescuing complete wrecks.
1. A modern cutter hull undecked and very dusty turned into a useful sailing cutter. This was found in a friend's garage.
2. An Elizabethan galleon. A complete wreck bought in a box of other junk at auction. This was turned into a colourful little ship as you can see from the before and after photographs.
3. A Folkboat hull found in a relative's attic. Built up and cased this made him very happy.
4. A very badly smashed-up passenger cargo boat, again bought at auction. This had a huge clockwork motor inside. The hull measured nearly three feet long. Completely built up again.

Modern cutter. The hull was found in a friend's garage. Seen here after decking over ready for rigging. (No.1)

Modern cutter. The finished boat. (No.1)

An Elizabethan galleon wreck bought at auction in a box of junk. Before reconstruction. (No.2)

The reconstructed Elizabethan galleon. (No.2)

A Folkboat sailer. The old hull was found in a relative's attic. She was decked out and fitted and put into a case. (No.3)

Passenger cargo boat circa 1930s. The finished model after complete reconstruction. (No.4)

Gangways and handrails

Gangways was the original name given to a fixed or movable planked platform on either side of the waist of the ship. This was a convenient way for the crews to get from the poop quarter deck to the forecastle deck without having to descend to the main deck. They came into use in about the middle of the 1750s (see Fig. 51, A). Other simple methods were used before this date. The illustration shows at (Fig. 51) frigate type decks of about 1780 (G & H). Fig. 52 shows a merchant ship of about 1850.

Skid beams across the waist of the hull supported the ship's boats and replacement spars (see Fig. 51, B & Fig. 52, C). Sometimes the gangways were just narrow planks supported by wooden crutch brackets on the bulwarks (see Fig. 52, D). A handrail gangway was fixed from the quarter deck to the skids (see Fig. 52, E).

Skid beams became fixed around the 1780s and attached under the gangway runs. In civil ships the skids were sometimes lifted higher on iron supports above the gunwale to make launching the boats easier (see Fig. 52, F).

The width of these waist gangways increased and by the middle of the 1800s covered the whole waist in some naval warships, forming another deck.

Be guided by your plan on gangways for their scale and positioning.

Handrails

These are easy to make as long as they are straight, curved are more difficult, as around bow and stern. Nails, pins and wooden pegs can be used here. If the scale of the model allows, curved sections of the rail can be cut with a knife or fretsaw. A small soldering iron is a useful tool in model boat-building, especially with metal handrails. Descriptions of various methods are shown later (see Fig. 52, G).

Deck equipment and furniture

This part of model ship building can be very absorbing, especially if you are good at converting the objects found in a workshop scrap box. Old clock pieces and electrical parts, wire of different gauges, washers and rivets can all be transformed into useful and effective pieces of equipment on the model's deck etc. You can buy these pieces as prepared castings or made up ones, but it will cost you more money and is certainly not so satisfying.

Starting with capstans and windlasses: a windlass is the horizontal version of the capstan. The capstan was the original way by which heavy hauling jobs were accomplished (see Fig. 53). Capstans were in use in the early 16th century and were developed into many different types. Some of the early ones were nothing more than a vertical log of wood, piercing the deck and set in a block of wood on the deck below (see Fig. 53, A). In the 18th century large warships had wooden ones, sometimes metal bound, on the top and lower decks, both connected by the same central core. Twice as many hands could be used when the heavy anchor cables were in use (see Fig. 53, B). Capstans were used on different parts of the deck — the heavy ones tended to be on or under the forecastle deck. Going aft of the ship's deck, lighter capstans were used for working drag anchors and rigging (see Fig. 53, D). Around the base of the metal capstans was a pawl ring with stops for the metal dogs, hinged at one end to fall against to prevent reverse winding under load (see Fig. 53, C). The single capstan was supported by a vertical core through the deck into a block bearing on the lower deck (see Fig. 53, C & D).

Model ship capstans are not difficult to make from dowel, cotton reels and some types of small bottle caps etc. We shall not be including all the minute detail in our efforts. Be guided by your plan or research in positioning these, with due regard to the scale.

The windlass was originally a horizontal log of hard wood, six- or eight-sided, held between two points. The log was pierced with staff holes around the two end peripheries to enable leverage with wooden or metal bars inserted in the holes. In the centre of the log deep V grooves were cut to enable a gravity type of latch, hinged at one end (the pawl), to fall into the grooves to prevent the log from turning back on itself. This was useful for the crew to rest in long hauls.

Winches were the natural progression from the windlass. Both types overlapped in history for many years. Some were geared and for lighter jobs they were directly driven with one or two crank handles. These were common features on 18th- and 19th-century ships for controlling lighter rigging or other minor hauling jobs (see Fig. 54, A). On some smaller, single-decked ships it was possible to mount the windlass barrel between two bitts fixed to opposite bulwarks near the bows. These supports were also known as Carrick bitts or windlass bitts (see Fig. 54, B). This is a naval cutter of 1760. The vertical post to the fore of the windlass barrel supported the pawl that fell into the central cog groove incision on the barrel when in a resting position. A more sophisticated windlass had a double rocker arm device with gravity pawl plate that slowly turned the barrel (see Fig. 54, C).

Making a windlass from sheets of ply or wood, even thick card, is not that difficult. The drum can be made from dowel or even an old stub of an unpainted pencil. It is six-sided and very convincing. Once painted in grey matt paint it looks good. Crank handles made of thickish copper wire serve the purpose well. The odd bolt head or screw head can be put in with a thin felt pen after painting the windlass. Clock cogs and axles make effective geared winches.

From the 19th century onwards the all-metal winch came into use, in many different patterns and patents (see Fig. 54, D).

Fig. 51.

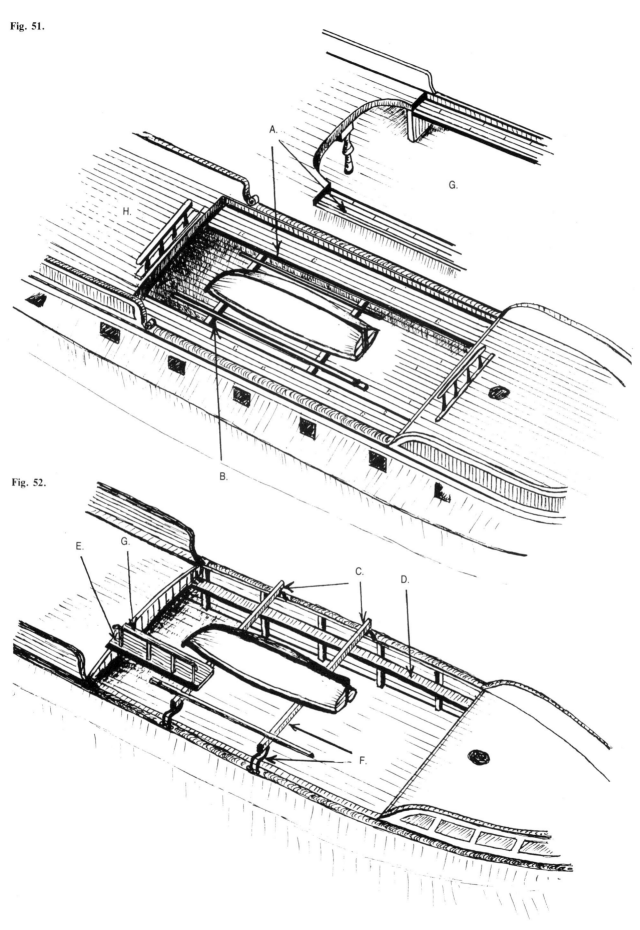

Fig. 52.

Three different types of ship's waist gangways.

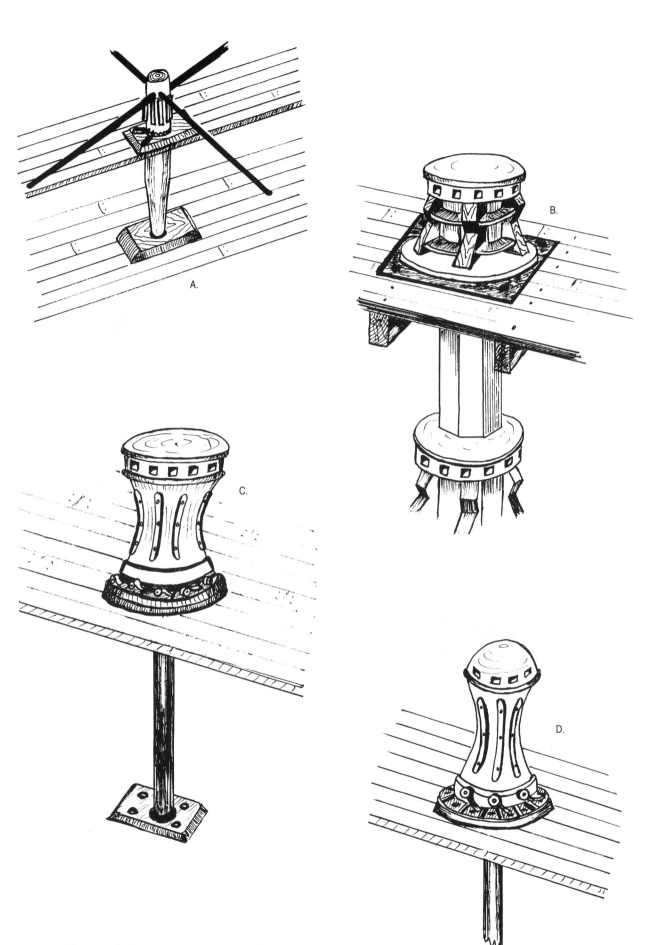

Fig. 53. Different period capstans.

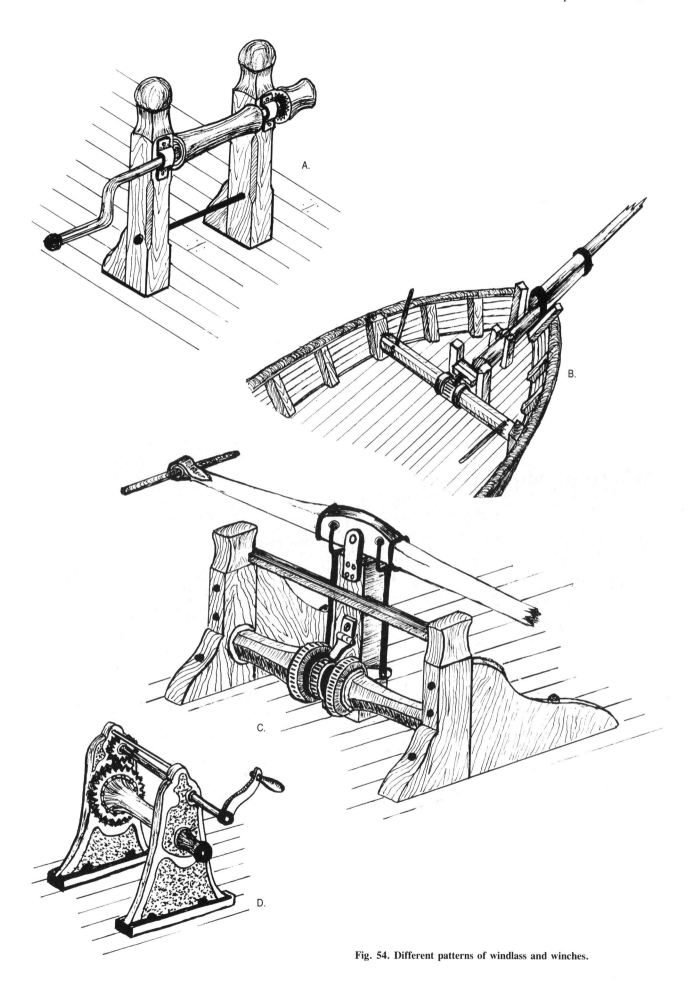

Fig. 54. Different patterns of windlass and winches.

The British coastal barge *Charlotte* circa 1900–1930.

This kind of model gives plenty of opportunity for deck detailing. Hatch covers, navigation lamps, pumps, winches and a small kiosk cabin aft. The hull was carved from the solid and would be a good simple shape for a beginner to start with. The rigging is not very difficult and there are plenty of good plans available of coastal and river barges.

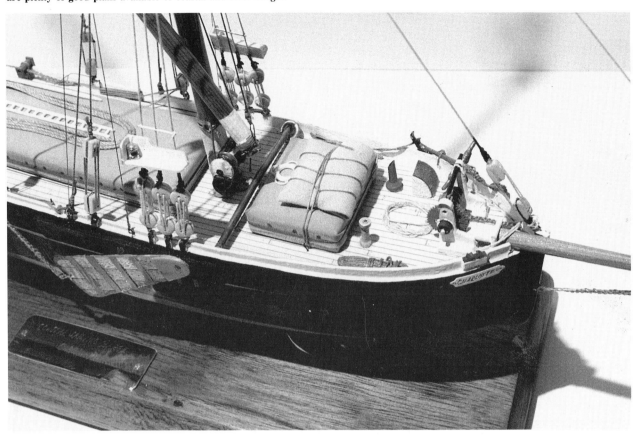

This picture shows the bow deck detail. Note the winch made up from old alarm clock cogs. Navigation oil lamps are mounted in a two-sided box fitted to the shroud lines just above the deadeyes.

A good view of the kiosk cabin that housed the steering gear. The ship's boat is in davits on the starboard side.

The finished model.

Hatches, skylights and davits

With this deck surface detail there is much to tax your imagination.

Hatches are openings in the ship's deck for crew or cargo. The covers that close the openings are hatch covers, sometimes boards for a cargo hatch and hinged lids or simple flaps, solid or glazed for the crew's ingress and egress.

Cargo hatches were battened down during passage, their tops and coamings covered with tarpaulins held in place with ropes (see Fig. 55, A). These were originally tan, grey, white or black coverings of painted, oiled or tarred canvas (see Fig. 55, E).

Wooden gratings were another feature of early deck openings for ventilation through decks. Shot garlands were sometimes found either side of the gratings (see Fig. 55, B & F).

Skylights in the 1700s were positioned over the poop deck. Often the captain's quarters were below this deck, a useful position in smaller ships where urgent communications were required between captain and helmsman. Skylight openings, if glazed, were heavily protected by brass or bronze bars (see Fig. 55, C). The skylights were sometimes joined with a companionway hood (see Fig. 55, D).

Hatches can be made from solid pieces of wood cut off a plank of the correct thickness. Cover them with a piece of material and tie with cord or cotton. Sometimes a little padding with cottonwool between wooden block and cover helps the effect when tied down.

I have used Paxilin circuit board perforated with small holes for gratings. These save a lot of patience. You can drill out a small sheet of wood and use a small square needle file if you have the patience!

One other method of producing a grating is to use cross-stitch canvas. This material comes in different gauges so have a look around the local needlework shops. Using the correct gauge for the model, cut a square to the correct size. Paint it matt brown and when dry stick down onto a piece of black card of the same size. Put a light weight onto the piece until dry. You can now stick the whole piece down onto your hatch cover block. This method is quite suitable and effective for the small type of model. You really will have to make the gratings from wood in the larger models.

When making a skylight — whether canted, a roof slope or flat — cut out of the solid first. For the glass effect I make sure the roof is smooth and then apply two coats of high gloss varnish over a black base paint. Then

Fig. 55.

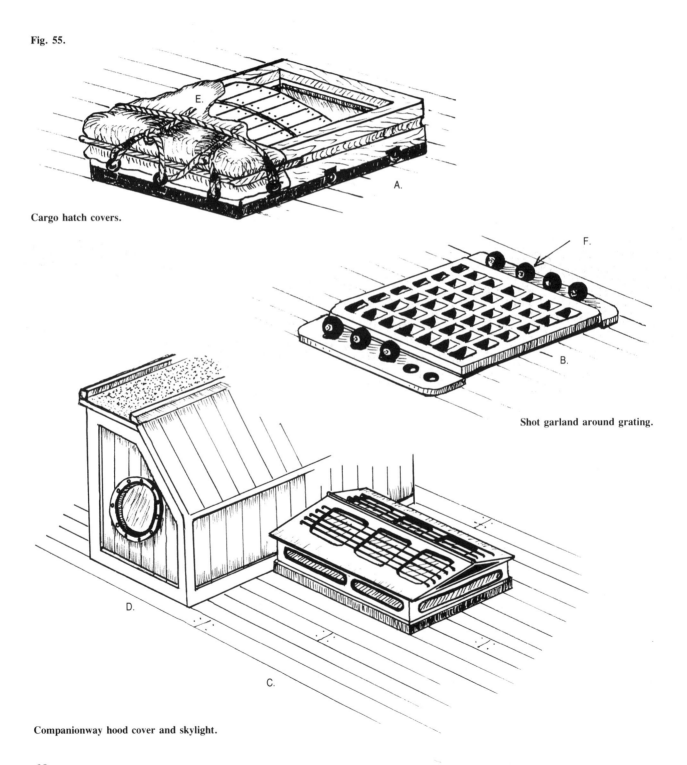

Cargo hatch covers.

Shot garland around grating.

Companionway hood cover and skylight.

using a sharp scalpel, cut out a pre-ruled card (business card thickness) to form the window frames or lights. This is now carefully stuck down onto the roof. This card is painted matt white or grey. The varnish gloss showing through looks exactly like a shiny glass window. Protecting bars can be stuck down wire across the windows.

Ship's boats

Some of the ship's boats, or sea boats are they were called, found on various types of sailing vessels are listed below. Good plans will indicate ship's boats in their details.

The captain's barge

This was called the 'second boat' on large sailing warships. A double-banked pulling boat with fourteen oars with mast and sail when needed. These were usually carvel built.

A gig

A light narrow ship's boat, built for speed originally, clinker built, rowing four to six single-banked oars.

Dinghy

A small open rowing boat, usually clinker built, pulling one pair of oars and used for general work and tendering.

Yawl

Up to the mid 19th century this term was used for any ship's boat rowed by four or more oars. Sometimes these craft had a foremast and small mizzen stepped abaft of the rudder-head.

Skiff

A ship's working boat, small and clinker built, pulling one or two pairs of oars. These were used for errands around the ship and when in harbour. All these types of ship's boats would be used as lifeboats when needed.

The lashings for ship's boats not fixed to davits, are very necessary to make safe the various rowing and sailing boats stowed on the ship's decks. These craft are usually mounted upright on blocks or stands with wedges of some sort. Being upright they collected water and this helped to keep the planks tight, especially in tropical latitudes. The illustration shows one method of roping down these boats, usually two sets of lashings and blocks were used. Show this detail by all means if the scale size allows. The method of tightening these lashings was by using double sets of deadeyes in early ships, these were replaced by double or single pulley blocks as in the illustration on this page viewed from the stern.

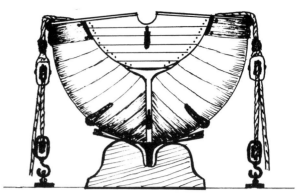

Ship's boat lashings.

Small trading vessels around the northern latitudes of the world could stow some of their smaller ship's boats upside down. There are many options for you to choose from when dealing with this important detail.

Davits

Davits were heavy beams of timber that held a ship's boat for lowering from the stern positions of some ships like sloops, brigs, schooners and naval ships (see Fig. 56).

Some davits were bolted onto the rail capping, other davit beams pierced the transom for stern boats. On some warships the davits were attached to the side of the stern deck near the mizzen shrouds, hinged at one end and controlled from above by pulley blocks (see Fig. 56, B).

Quarter boats were used from these suspension points (safety boats for quick launching). These boats were in addition to those stowed in the ship's waist.

Warships tended to set all ships' boats adrift or tow them in battle. Cannon fire would smash boats into flying shards of timber which could seriously injure the crew. The boats adrift were used by both sides of a conflict when ships went down! Metal davits came into use around the 1860s. These were held on the inside of the bulwarks and could revolve so that the ship's boat could be suspended either inboard or outboard (see Fig. 56, D).

Channels and chainplates

'Chain wales' was the original name for the channels. These were timbers set below gunwale level enabling the shrouds to clear the side of the ship so distributing the pressure exerted by the mast shrouds to the side of the ship. The chainplates, referred to as 'chains', were the means by which the shrouds were attached to the side of the hull (see Fig. 57, D).

The chainplates were originally iron loops resembling chains. By the mid 1700s they were becoming long double loops of iron or straight bars (see Fig. 57, F &

Fig. 56. Different types of davits.

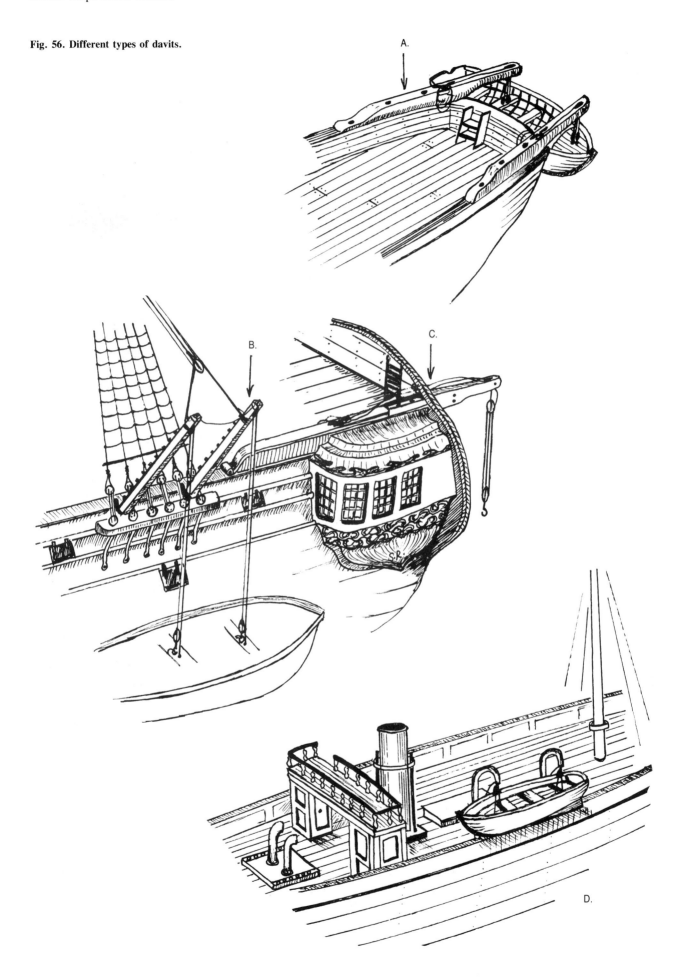

A three-masted Barque — circa 1890.

The set of plans for this model showed no name for the vessel so I called it *Emma Hope*.

Until the mid-19th century, barques were relatively small sailing ships, but later were built up to about 3,000 tons. These were used for the grain and nitrate trades. Four and even five-masted ships were later built. The Americans call them barks, never barque.

There are many good contemporary photos of these vessels, so if you are researching prior to making a model from plans there is plenty of material available.

Deck area.

The finished model.

H). From the bolted position on the side of the hull they were notched into the edge of the channel, terminating on the top side of the channel with a deadeye (see Fig. 57, A, E, F & J). Depending on the period this equipment took on many different patterns. Like so many things maritime, the approximate date of a vessel can often be judged by the fittings and equipment.

When making the channels choose a fine-grained hard wood. Cut it slightly over-width shown on plan so that you can shape it to the very slight curve in the hull. Do not notch it until it is stuck and pinned on the hull, because when it is fixed you will need to know the exact angle at which the chainplates are to be attached to the hull side. To do this is simple. If you have completed the masts, fit them into their respective holes in the deck, if not just use a piece of dowel. Adjust the angle of the mast by looking at the plan. Tie some thin cord or cotton to the position on the mast where the main shrouds will eventually be attached. With a pencil ready, angle the cord at each shroud position on the channel board edge and the hull below and draw a well defined line on the hull marking the edge of the channel board. This will now give you the exact angle for the chainplates, also the notch position on the edge of the channel board where the top of the chainplate will eventually rest (see Fig. 57, I). When finished, cap along the edge of the channel edge.

The different types and the ways chainplates were fitted to the hull are shown (see Fig. 57, G & H and Fig. 58, A to D).

We will not be making these with all the detail. Simple pieces of wire or thin strips of sheet metal will suffice. More on this later in the book.

Deadeyes

These were circular blocks of wood, usually made of lignum vitae or elm. We shall use a hard wood here — walnut, holly or boxwood if you can get some (see Fig. 57, J). These blocks were grooved around the circumference and pierced with three holes and were used in pairs to secure the end of a shroud to the chainplate. A rope lanyard was threaded through the holes in the deadeyes thus giving a purchase to tighten the shrouds (see Fig. 58, E). Another type of deadeye with only a single hole through it and called a heart was used to set up permanent stays.

The deadeye eventually made way for the bottlescrew to tighten shrouds and other set-up rigging about the 1860s (see Fig. 58, D).

Model shops dealing with model ship kits and materials can supply finished deadeyes in wood or cast plastic. These are usually ready to use and come in various sizes. They may only cost five pence or more each but you are going to need something like 40 to 50 of these for a three-masted vessel. A similar problem of quantity arises with pulley blocks. Here the numbers needed may

be even higher. More of this later. See Fig. 61, A to P — this is a selection of many other things you will find on the deck of a ship.

I have tried many different ways of making deadeyes — solid plastic rods, hardwood dowels and a small plug cutter bit in an electric drill. I found the best method after I had set up an old mixer motor with a chuck.

Prepare a piece of very well seasoned hardwood by planing roughly into the round. The diameter should be very near to the finished deadeye size. Taper one end down to a size to fit the chuck jaws. I support the other end of the rod by pushing it into a hole drilled in a block of wood, the same height as the chuck jaws — this is a very primitive lathe. If you have a proper lathe then use this.

Take a sharp pencil or Biro and switch on the motor. Mark off the individual deadeyes to the correct thickness, going back over them and marking in the individual grooves.

Take a small V-shaped file and cut in the grooves with the chuck still revolving. Then with a fine saw (model maker stiff-backed type) carefully cut between each deadeye. Do not cut right through, about a quarter will do. Take the rod out of the chuck and finish cutting the deadeyes apart with the saw. Sandpaper each side. Mark for each of the three holes and drill with the small model-maker's drill. A good tip is to have a small board drilled to the depth and circumference of your deadeye. Pop them into the board before drilling. This keeps them in place and avoids drilling through your finger!

However you may find it difficult to obtain a really fine-grained hardwood suitable for deadeyes. Large-gauge plastic knitting needles of around 6½mm are most useful. Hand-cut slices of the correct thickness with a handsaw that you can fit fine fretsaw blades into is the way to prepare these plastic deadeyes. As this type of plastic is grainless and not brittle you can drill the three holes without splitting. Sand lightly on either side and make a couple of groove cuts around the edge of the deadeye. This should be sufficient to hold the fixing around the deadeye.

The standard knitting needle is grey but takes inks or dyes quite well if you want to colour the finished piece.

If your eyesight isn't too good when threading the lanyards through the deadeyes, get a small needle threader which is sold for getting the cotton through a sewing machine needle. You will find this little gadget invaluable.

Rudders and steering gear

Originally steering was accomplished by using a steer-board (starboard side, the right side) suspended and held over the side of the vessel's stern. Steering equipment is known generally as the helm. About the 14th century the centre line rudder with gudgeons and pintle hingeing was developed. Control was by a tiller bar which went

Fig. 57.

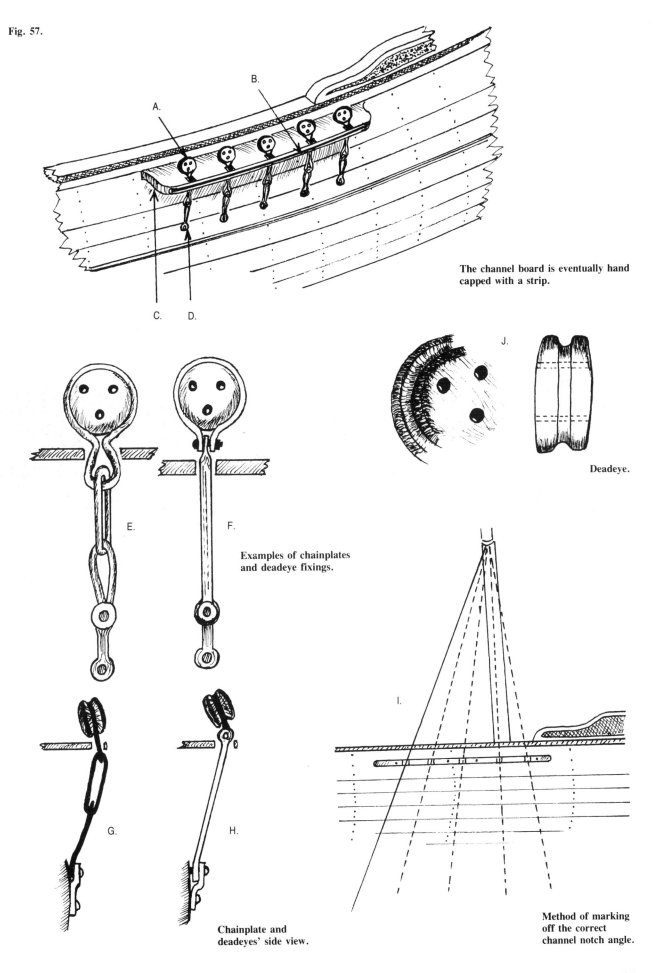

A.

B.

The channel board is eventually hand capped with a strip.

C.   D.

J.

Deadeye.

E.   F.

Examples of chainplates and deadeye fixings.

I.

G.   H.

Chainplate and deadeyes' side view.

Method of marking off the correct channel notch angle.

65

Fig. 58.

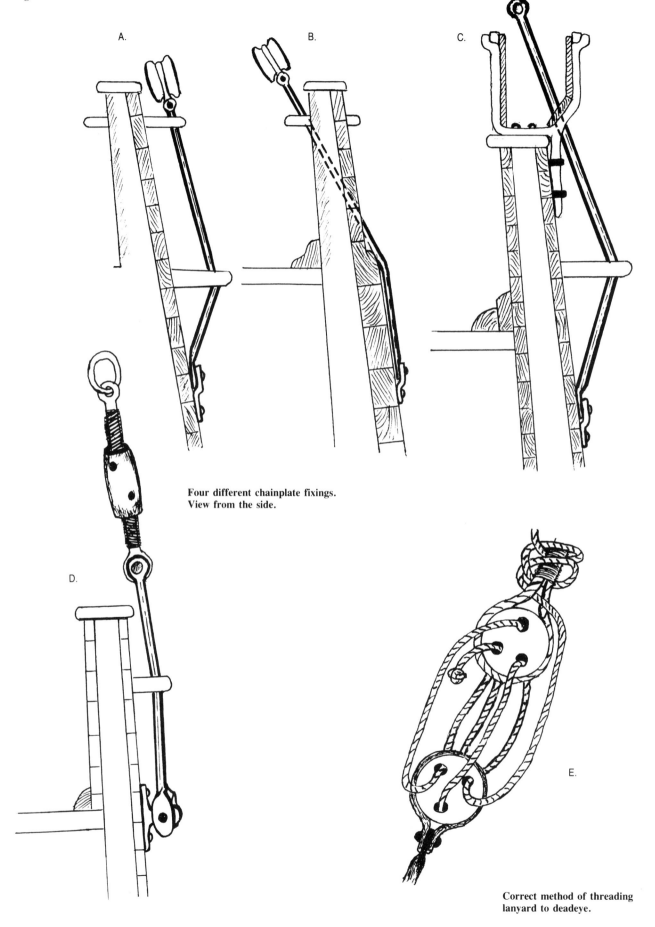

A.

B.

C.

**Four different chainplate fixings.
View from the side.**

D.

E.

**Correct method of threading
lanyard to deadeye.**

through a horizontally slotted hole in the ship's transom. The rudder board top held the tiller. In heavy weather this caused problems of swamping with water entering the main deck at the stern. As decks became higher in the poop area the helmsman found it more difficult to see where he was going and the whipstaff was developed. This connected with the tiller bar below enabling the helmsman to be positioned on a higher deck. He could also apply greater leverage to the helm and his vision was much improved (see Fig. 59, A, B, C, & D).

After 1700 the rudder post was extended upwards through the overhanging counter which improved the flooding problem. By the mid-1700s the rudder posthead took on a circular or rounded square shape. The post angle was changed so that it was in line with the pintles enabling the post to revolve in a closely fitting hole. The tiller arm could now be controlled by rope and pulley (yoke lines). The ultimate development was the steering wheel on the deck above (see Fig. 59, E).

Be guided by the plan when making and fitting the rudder. With static ship models the rudder is set in a central position and can be fixed permanently.

Thin slithers of wood, metal or card can be stuck onto the finished rudder board and sternpost to simulate strengthening bands, pintles and gudgeons. When painted these can be picked out in a slightly different colour and look convincing. I sometimes use very thin tin or sheet copper for this and apply the pieces to the rudder assembly with Araldite glue. After this part is finished you can peg with fine headless nails or pins and a dab of glue onto the sternpost. If your ship is single decked and the helm is controlled directly by tiller bar only, remember to fix the rudder post above deck level in a vertical line with the rudder top. In larger models you may choose to drill through the stern, as in reality, for the rudder post.

Fife rails

These belaying points are to be found in ships of all periods, mostly at the base of masts. Some had sheaves in the upright posts. On schooners they tended to follow the angle of masts which were canted quite a bit (see Fig. 60, A). Other types were like horseshoes and some were just straight bars (see Fig. 60, B & C). At the base of some masts strong metal bands with protruding ring bolts provided more points to belay lighter rigging lines. The belaying pins were distributed along the fife rail (see Fig. 60, D).

The making of fife rails is pretty straightforward using small pieces of hardwood. Anything from about ¼″ square or smaller suits the average scale of model ship. Try and drill the rail for the belaying pins before you assemble and glue. With small models the upright posts can just be glued on the deck surface. Larger models may need you to set the uprights in small holes in the deck and glue well in. It is surprising the strain put onto

these fife rails when you rig the ship. It looks good to have taut rigging where it should be. A little over-enthusiasm with a cord can lift right off your carefully placed fife rail. It's happened to me more than once! This applies to all belaying points throughout the model, so be warned.

The anchor

There have been whole books written just about the different types of anchor from the simple lump of stone (the Killick) to the multitude of metal types that followed. We shall concentrate on the standard type being used from about 1780 onwards. Some of the earlier English patterns had V-shaped arms and not the curved arms most of us are familiar with.

The shank of the anchor (see Fig. 62, C) was usually squared off towards the top. This enabled the stock (see Fig. 62, A) to be fitted, usually in two slabs, either side of the shank. The side view plan shows that it was tapered. Heavy wrought metal bands were knocked on to the stock — the tighter they became, the better the stock gripped the shank preventing any movement.

Your plan or your own research might give you the type of anchor to be fitted to your model, if not fit the type illustrated. This pattern lasted for many years, some later ones were the same shape but made completely of wrought iron.

Soldering the metal pieces together after shaping (if you choose not to buy a model anchor) is the best way to proceed. Composite anchors made from any softish metal and wood are the easiest. Casting them from plastic epoxy filler pressed into a pre-carved hardwood mould is another possibility. Most anchors when finished should end up dark in colour, black or dark rusty colour. You will need two at least. These were mounted near the bows of the ship or catted to the side ready to drop when needed (see Fig. 62, H to L).

Prior to about the 1840s large ship anchors were usually stowed outside the bulwarks, tied off on the channel or with the fluke hooked over the bulwark rail. Later anchors were brought inboard. 'Billboards' covered the exterior planking as protection against chaffing by the anchor flukes, these were sometimes referred to as 'Bills', hence billboards (see Fig. 62, G, H, I, J & K). In G this is a clipper of about 1870. In H, this is a naval ship of 1780. In I this shows a smaller ship of the 1700s and in K another small ship sporting a curved cathead of grown timber. In J you will see the cathead is carved, sometimes as a star or a lion. Unless the model is very large do not bother with this embellishment — it will hardly show. Catheads were sheaved with two or three pulleys. Hanging from these were the cat blocks with large hooks to the anchor ring.

You will again have to be guided by your plans for these important items at the bows of the model. Hardwood should be used making sure that the edges of the pieces

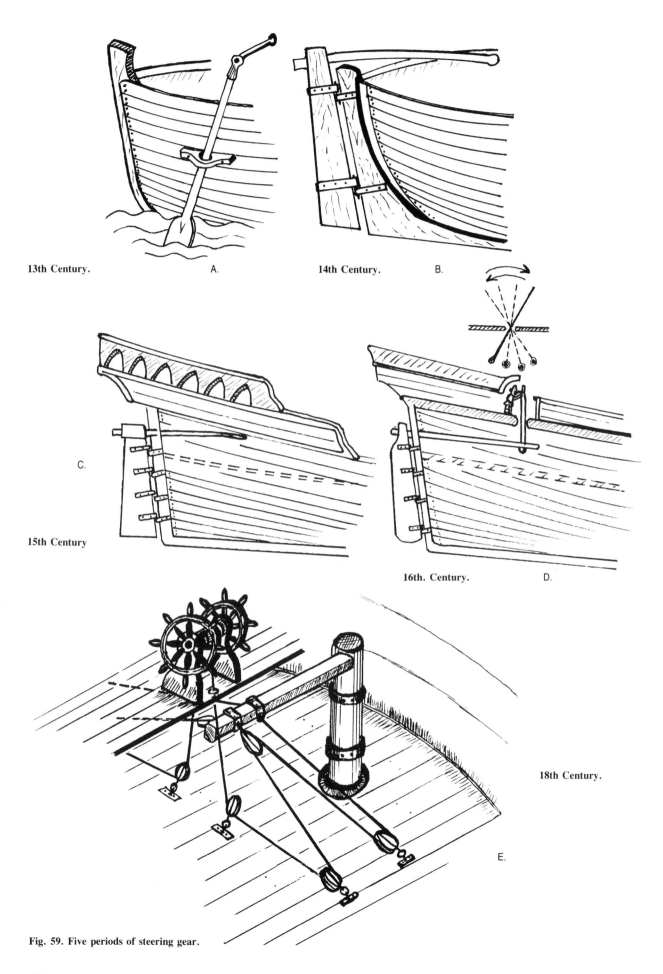

13th Century.   A.   14th Century.   B.

C.
15th Century

                                                        16th. Century.   D.

                                                                    18th Century.

                                                                    E.

Fig. 59. Five periods of steering gear.

Fig. 60.

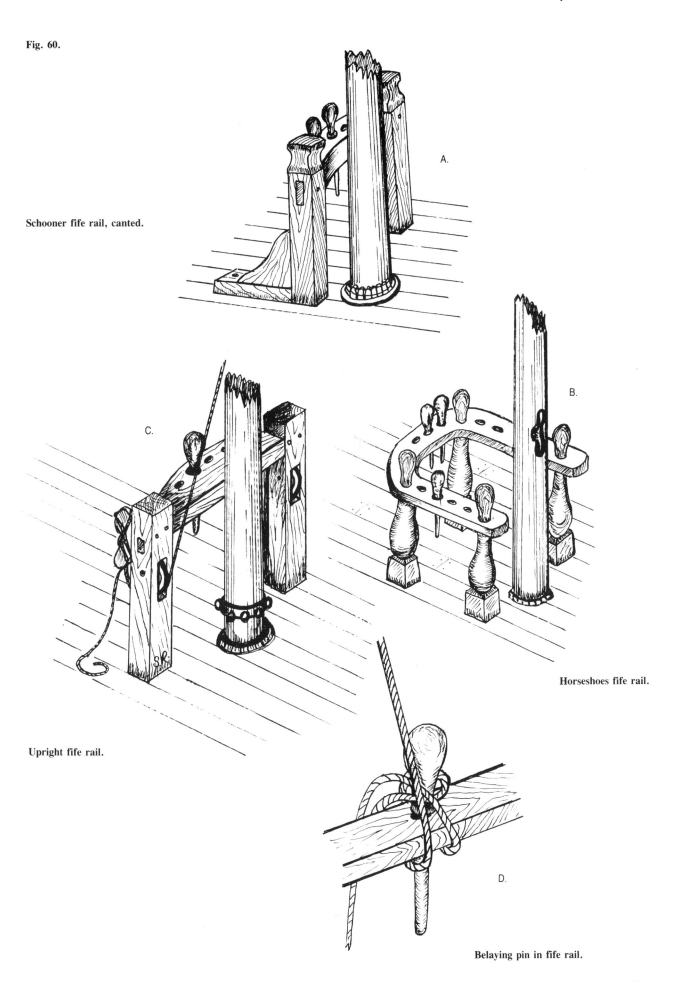

A.

Schooner fife rail, canted.

B.

C.

Horseshoes fife rail.

Upright fife rail.

D.

Belaying pin in fife rail.

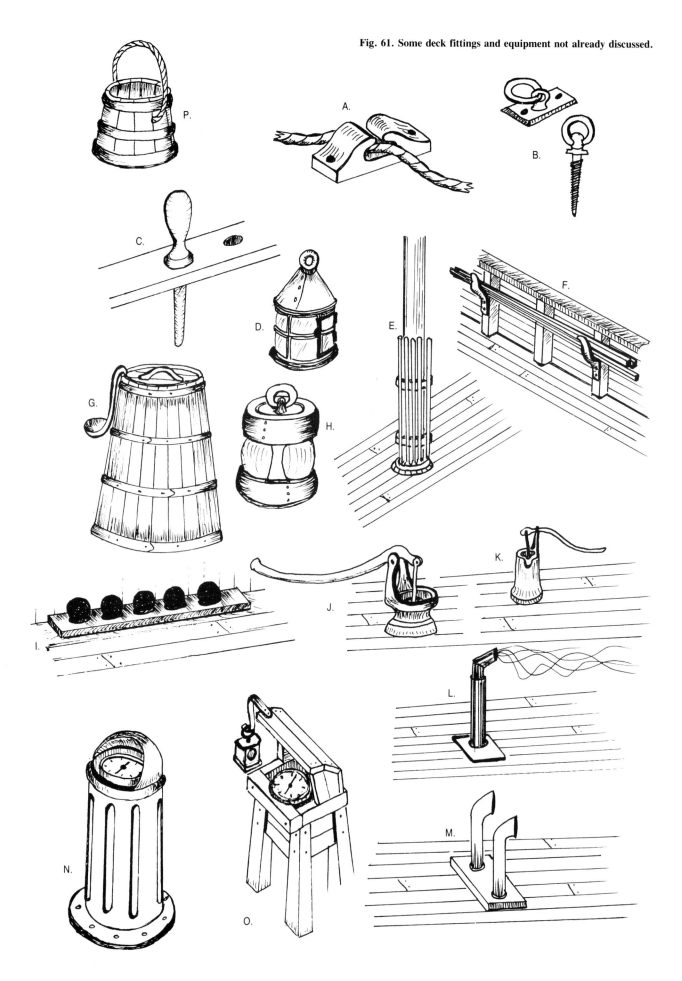

Fig. 61. Some deck fittings and equipment not already discussed.

A. *Fairlead*	The means by which a rope or cable is led at a slightly different angle or kept in place at deck or bulwark level.
B. *Ring bolts*	These can be screw type or attached to a plate.
C. *Belaying pins*	Found along racks on bulwarks, usually at foot of shroud lines and also fife rails at base of masts.
D. & H. *Lanterns & lamps*	Various types depending on period or use. For navigation etc.
E. & F. *Capstan & winch bars*	These should be stowed near the equipment, around the mast or on horizontal racks at bulwarks.
G. *Drinking water butt*	These were lidded and a drinking ladle hung from the barrel lip.
I. *Shot racks or garlands*	Found at edges of hatchways and bulwark bottoms in the 1850s. Earlier, shot was stacked in small pyramids held in wooden frames at deck centres.
J. & K. *Deck level pumps*	Usually mounted in smaller ships on the deck centrally in the waist of the ship, above the bilges' lowest point.
L. *Galley smoke stack*	From the galley stove below deck. Usually bent at top facing aft.
M. *Ventilation shafts and ducts*	With the advent of steam these were introduced and in full use by 1860s on new steam and sail ships.
N. & O. *Binnacles*	A wooden housing for the ship's compass near the helm position (prior 1800s). Later made of bronze or brass. Many different patterns.
P. *Buckets*	These were usually leather or cooper made, bound with wood strip or metal banded. Rope handles were knotted through the sides.

you prepared are finished sharp edged and not rounded, unless the plan states otherwise.

Hammock nettings

These were strange but distinctive features on ships of the 18th and 19th centuries. The original netting frames were attached just above the waist gangway, the poop and forecastle bulwarks in naval ships and East Indiamen. The gangway nettings were deeper than those found elsewhere on the ship. A double line of wrought iron bars formed the netting frame (see Fig. 63, A). The crew would roll up their blankets inside their sleeping hammocks, fold them double and each morning bring them to the nettings and stow them, so forming a tight wall within the netting. Apart from giving the bedding a fairly rigorous airing it had many uses, mainly protection in battle to absorb splinters and musket balls. On a sinking ship the hammock rolls would float out and could support a man for a few hours in the water if necessary.

A wooden rail was sometimes fitted inboard of the netting frame. The iron frames were portable but towards the 1880s canvas covers were fitted on the outside of the nettings and painted, giving the structure a more permanent look. Wood replaced the canvas coverings and more patent types of iron framing were used as on the C.S.S. *Alabama* built for the Confederate government by Laird of Liverpool in 1862 (see Fig. 63, B). Although these were now hollow boxes for the stowage of hammocks and canvas in general, they were still referred to as hammock nettings.

Notes on painting

We have come quite a long way in describing the scratch-built model ship. The order of painting is some-thing that should go on from the beginning. When you can see that it would be difficult to paint an area as more detail is added, paint as you go. The inside of the bulwark for instance, and the colouring of the deck are good examples. Masts, yards, and the tops should be dealt with early on. Sometimes the doubling of the masts were painted white or grey with the rest of the mast left natural but varnished.

Always try to use matt or semi-matt colours unless there is a good reason to use a gloss, as on some hull exteriors. Mast and spar bands should always be painted as they are finished and before they are fitted. The same applies to all metal work and deck fittings.

General model paints are the best type to use as long as they are not too thick. They come in a good range of colours and finishes. You will only need about 3 or 4 brush sizes. I use cheap water-colour brushes, the largest size for the hull exterior.

The correct colour to paint the hull can be a little mystifying. Most of the 18th-century warships had dark, usually black, exteriors, for the most part above the water-line. The inside areas of the bulwarks were painted red so as not to show the blood that inevitably flowed in battle.

The hull sheer line was often picked out in buff colour above and below the gunports externally. Merchantmen of the period often chequered the exterior of bulwarks alternately with buff or white against the black of the hull. At a distance this gave the impression of gunports.

A darkish tone of green was a well-used colour on working boats both in Great Britain and America. It was thought to be the best wearing colour to put on a boat. The Old Block Island boats and Pinkys of America were painted in this fashion with a white or light colour sheer line. Below the water-line hot pitch was applied before the advent of copper paints.

Decks tended to be light in colour due to the bleaching effect of sun and the continuous use of holystone and sand to scrub decks clean, with black pitch caulking between the planks.

Fig. 62.

**Standard pattern anchor,
18th–19th Century.**

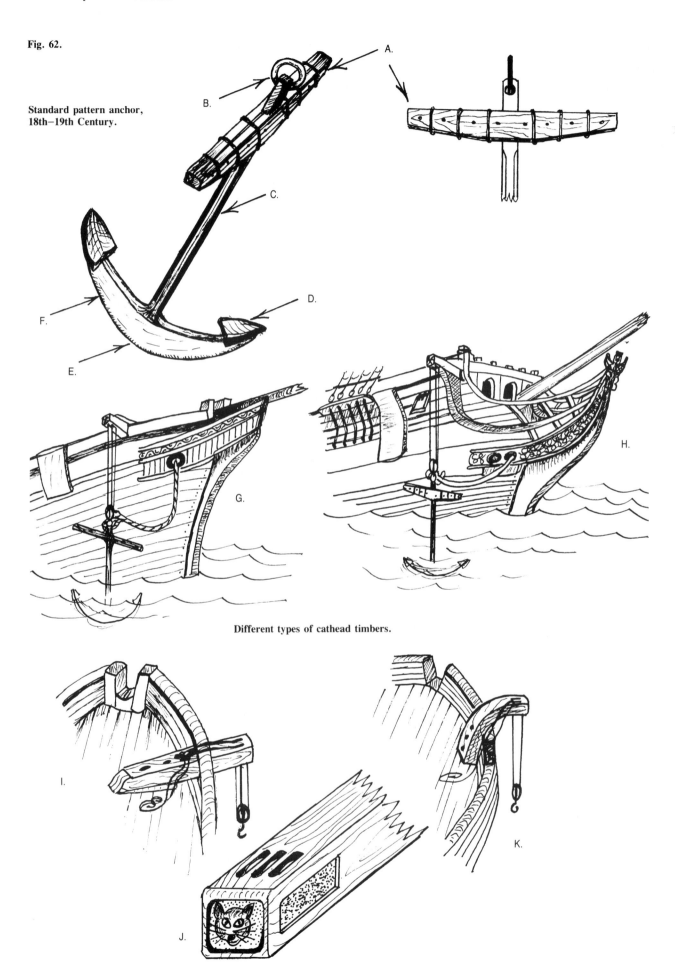

Different types of cathead timbers.

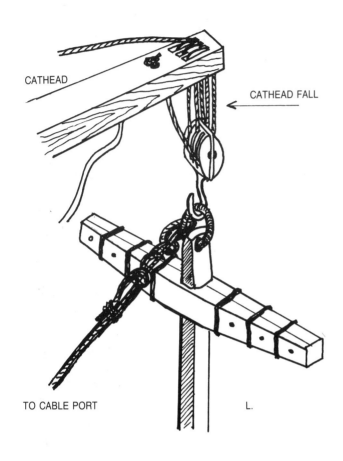

CATHEAD

CATHEAD FALL

TO CABLE PORT   L.

hues in the 18th and early 19th centuries.

HMS *Victory*, built in 1765, is beautifully restored and lies in her docks at Portsmouth, England. Her hull sides have alternate bands of black and buff, her masts are buff with iron bands in black. The doors to the exterior of the peak head deck are picked out in a bright blue and there is much gilding. This old ship of Nelson's times contrasts well with the sombre but extremely smart look of the black and white colouring of HMS *Warrior* built in the 1860s, which lies nearby in the same dockyard. This steam and sailing warship (similar in looks to the C.S.S. *Alabama*)is painted mostly in white internally and black externally, with odd parts in buff and black and small amounts of gilding.

Ships' boats mounted on decks and stern davits give you the opportunity of a little more contrast with interiors perhaps in white, buff or grey. Exteriors were mid-green or earthy colours.

Just remember that like the sails, if made badly, will spoil the best model ships, so will careless painting!

Utilizing old model soldiers and other figures in metal or plastic, dare I say, is one way of solving the figure-head requirement if your model shop cannot help.

Flags, pennants and various standards make for a colourful and attractive finish to your model ship but be careful to get it correct for the period and type of ship. The British Navy sported the Cross of St. George in Elizabethan times. With the Union this changed to the Union Jack. To this was added three types of ensigns — Red, Blue and White. In America around the 1860s the flag was changing, so do not forget to count the number of stars!

You may be able to buy these various flags but it's more fun to make them on thin paper using poster or watercolour paints, so try your hand here.

Rigging

Rigging embraces all ropes, wire and chains used in ships to support the masts and to control the yards, booms, gaffs and sails. All the rigging used in support of masts, bowsprit and yards is known generally as standing rigging. It is rarely removed and does not run through blocks. Because of its standing state it is preserved with paints, tars or tar varnishes. On our model a semi-matt or eggshell finish in black is used on this type of rigging.

Running rigging is everything else that is needed to move yards, trim sails and control booms and gaffs etc.

We shall start with the mast support rigging, then the bowsprit and jib boom and finally the mizzen, most of which is best described with the illustrations (see Figs. 38 and 39).

One very important fact to remember is to try and get all cordage to the correct scale for the ship and the job it is supposed to do. Also be careful to get the colours correct.

Rich captains could afford plenty of gilding on the gingerbread detailing and carving on prow and poop. Some model shops will supply plain moulded decoration ready for applying to hull and gilding. You can often find gilded picture frames from which you can prize off mouldings to utilize. Look around your local junk shop for decorative sheet brass door furniture etc. This works well when painted with gold paint after snipping into shape.

The correct colouring for the period of ship you are working on is best researched. Keep a few notes if you visit museums and maritime establishments where models of old ships are displayed.

Fourteenth- and fifteenth-century ships were extremely colourful with chequered designs in many colours and coats of arms just about everywhere along the exteriors of their hulls. This preoccupation with multi-colours and much gold leaf carried on into the eighteenth century for countries like Spain. The British and American ships, however, became more conservative regarding colour, except for gilding the ornamentation on stem figure-heads and stern.

Bright colours were very expensive before the advent of synthetic colours so the large navies tended to use the early pigments like drab reds, yellows, oranges and buff

The Pinky *Eagle* 1820.

A very American sailing boat, the Pinky type, with its design roots in the Mediterranean like the feluccas. These boats were built in the parish of Chebacco in the town of Ipswich before the American revolution (now the town of Essex, Massachusetts). They were used as fast fishing boats on the nearby banks. After the revolution some of them turned to privateering!
These are easy models to make having a very economic rigging plan and simple deck layout.

Fig. 63.

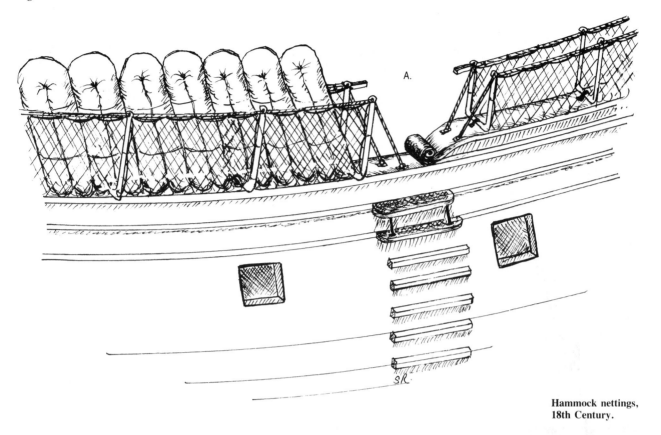

Hammock nettings, 18th Century.

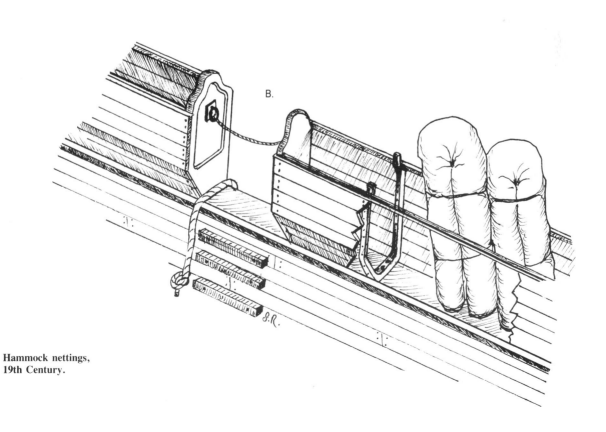

Hammock nettings, 19th Century.

C.S.S. *Alabama*.

A very interesting ship to make as a model. ASP Plans service has a very good plan. The Confederate steamship was made by the British builder Laird Bros. Birkenhead. Launched June 1862 she sailed to the Azores to avoid being impounded by the British authorities for violating the Foreign Enlistment Act.

During the 22 months of her active service as a Confederate cruiser of the southern States she covered 75,000 miles, sunk, destroyed or ransomed some sixty four prizes before being sunk herself by the *Kearsarge*. Her wreck lies just three miles off Cherbourg.

Rigging the *Alabama*, carefully drilling with a hand chuck drill.

The *Alabama* with the first two ship's boats fitted and some rigging in place.

The foredeck of *Alabama* before adding more ratlines.

The stern of *Alabama* showing the small stern boat.

My first attempt at making the *Alabama*. Decks were ruled in on this model.

The second model of *Alabama* showing a planked-in deck. Compare this with the ruled-in deck of the first model of this ship.

Finished Models in Colour

This is a Brixham trawler of about the turn of the century. The hull is solid and the ship is a good type for the beginner to start with.

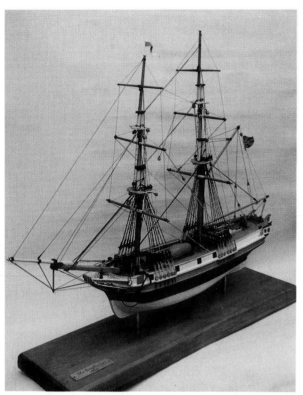

The Brig Neilson. **The finished model.**

The coastal barge *Emma* circa 1900.

Catalan boat 1440.

The *Rose Dorothea* 1906. The finished model.

C.S.S. *Alabama* 1862-64.

H.M.S. Frigate *Raleigh* **1776. Ex-American Navy.**

Passenger Cargo Boat circa 1930s.
This finished model was a badly smashed-up wreck found at auction. This is how she looked when finished and painted.

This is the original model of *Alabama* I made to illustrate the article that appeared in *Model Boats* Jan. 1988.

This is the Mk II version of the model.

Good model shops will supply ship model cordage in different types and colours. Try to avoid using ordinary strings of different gauges without preparing it first by colouring. Look around your local sewing and knitting shop. Carpet binding thread and heavy duty cotton threads can be used in some rigging jobs. Builders' lines, the sort used by bricklayers, made of cotton or hemp can be used for the heavier cordage when suitably prepared. Avoid rayons, nylons and other obviously synthetic cordage for your model ships — they are too glossy and never looks convincing.

Making some of your own cordage and rope is worth considering if you are not satisfied with what is available at the model supply shop.

Shroud ropes and mainstays are some of the thickest ropes on historical sailing ships. As they are thicker they are more visible to the critical eye. As already mentioned, hemp or cotton brick builders' lines with their strong and visible lay are very useful for the larger model shrouds when coloured properly. The smaller models of between twenty- and fifteen-inch hull lengths can be a problem as this scale of shroud cordage seems difficult to simulate.

Thick carpet thread, crochet cotton and other types of thread can be twisted together. Take a hand-twist drill and put a small hook into the chuck. Get two or three equal lengths of the material you are going to use — I work with six to ten foot lengths. Tie the lines onto the hook, then secure the other ends of the cord, checking each has equal tension by pulling the drill taut. Start twisting the drill until the twist on the lines has reached the correct look of a shroud rope. With the geared drill this takes only a few seconds.

Get a large blob of PVA wood glue on a pad of rag and on the tensioned line rub along the entire length of the twisted line keeping the tension high. Leave until dry, then cut each end and wind onto a reel ready for use. The glue is to prevent the obvious bird's nest effect that would happen after twisting once the tension is released.

This type of home-laid cordage really works well and looks very convincing as scaled down real rope.

Spare cordage and ropes that are to be found neatly coiled or flaked down on decks add to the reality aboard your model ship. Neat coils look good and if you use a backing of wetted gummed paper this will hold the coil in place. Start from the centre and coil around until you have a neat circle of rope. Trim off the gummed paper to the outer edge of the coil. You can now position the rope and glue down onto the deck. Sheet ropes should be looped on belaying pins. Before doing this, lightly glue the length. This takes any spring out of the cord and helps to set the loop or bunches of cordage.

A final note about cordage. Cordage over one inch in diameter was referred to as rope. Hemp, manila, sisal and coir (the husk of coconut, light enough to float but a quarter the strength of manila) was used in its manufacture. The different rope materials were used because of their natural qualities and characteristics such as hardness and springiness. They were twisted (laid) in different ways to make full use of these characteristics. Their colours varied from grey/white, straw colour, pale and dark brown to black when preserved like standing mainstays.

Rigging chains can be made from the types of light chains supplied by the do-it-yourself jewellery and craft shops. This comes in steel or brass-coated lengths and can be lightly painted providing you thin out the colouring agent first so as to avoid blocking the chain links.

When beginning to rig your ship try and do it in some kind of order. It is so easy to get involved in one part of the ship and forget some of the work that should be completed first. Remember to work from either side alternately. There are no hard rules but experience will lead you to your own formula. It's not much fun fighting your way through completed shrouds and ratlines to get to the fife rail or some other detail you have forgotten on deck.

Try and mount the completed masts into the deck first in models up to 2 feet long, making sure the hull is in some kind of working cradle and level as it would be if afloat. You may like to put a temporary water-line on your model beforehand (see Fig. 64, A). Make sure the line is horizontal then, checking your plan, set the masts at their correct angle. I usually glue mine at this point.

On the larger models various builders adopt a different order. The larger scale will allow those with patience to rig their ships 'almost for real', whipping every piece of rope and making every shroud loop, fixing them over the lower mast top before mounting the top mast into the cap and so on up to the top galliant. It depends on the time you have available and your patience. After all it's only a hobby!

I usually start by putting on one shroud line, cut long enough to thread it through the first top, over the quadrant bolster and between the doubling of masts and down the other side. Assuming your hull has all its chainplates topped with a deadeye and at the correct angle, you can attach the shroud line deadeye to the deck end of the shroud (see Fig. 64, B & C).

By using the little gadget described in the illustration, made from piano wire or two nails in a piece of plywood, fix one shroud to the chainplate on one side with its lanyard and then measure the shroud on the other side. Attach the deadeye making sure that when both sides are taut the deadeyes are exactly the same height above the bulwark rail. Thread the other lanyard as previously described (see Fig. 58, E) and tighten both sides by their lanyards and tie off making sure your mast is still at the correct angle and in line with the others. Also check if you have chosen, say, the foremast as a start, that both shroud lines are attached to their opposite number on either side of the hull. When the lanyards are tightened, the distance between the top and bottom deadeye should be approximately 4 to 5 deadeye diameters. A sheer pole is fitted above the top deadeyes

Fig. 64.

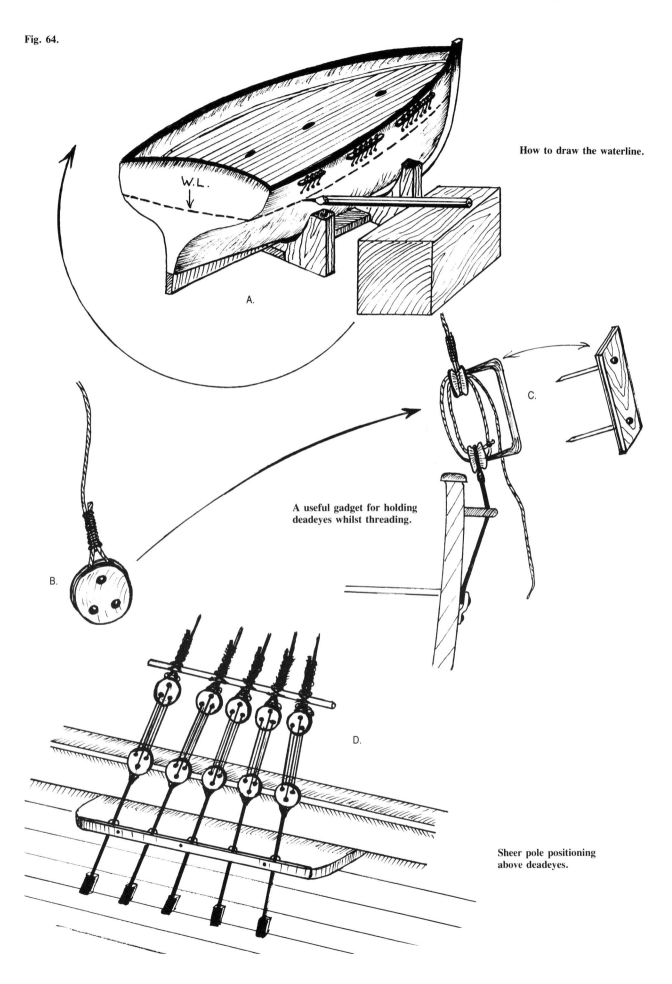

How to draw the waterline.

W.L.

A.

C.

A useful gadget for holding
deadeyes whilst threading.

B.

D.

Sheer pole positioning
above deadeyes.

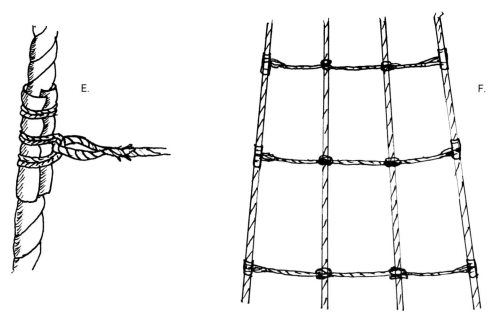

Fig. 64 *continued.*

In reality ratlines that formed the ladder for sailors on the shroud ropes had an eye on each and were seized to outermost shrouds. The intermediate fixing was a clove hitch. I make all the fixings of ratlines by clove hitch only, on each of the shrouds. A little blob of wood glue on each of the outermost lines secures these quite well. Forget the parcelling of shrouds — you would not see it on normal scale models.

(see Fig. 64, D).

The number of shroud lines and their chainplate attachments usually decrease in numbers as you move towards the stern. In some large sailing ships you may have as many as 10 or 12 on the foremast, 8 or 9 on the main and 4 or 6 on the mizzen. These numbers are on both sides of course. On smaller vessels the numbers are considerably reduced. See Fig. 64, E for ratline detail on shroud lines.

You may choose to fit one pair of shroud lines per mast to start with and carry on from there. If you have done this you can make a start on the bowsprit. It is helpful to change around on some of the more boring or difficult jobs and will improve your patience!

A final word regarding the shrouds and the way each individual rope is attached at the mast, or appears to be attached. There are two ways to do this. I follow the lazy way (see Fig. 65, A) on small models. The correct way is shown (see Fig. 65, B).

You may find that by the time you are threading the 4th or 5th shroud over the mast it will be a very tight fit if the topmast is fitted. This was often the case in reality. The bottom end of the topmast was cut, so reducing the thickness of the butt end near the fid hole (see Fig. 65, G).

Do not rush the rigging work. If you have not made any pulley blocks this is a good time to make some from hardwood. Look at your rigging plan and count the numbers you will need (see Fig. 75, A). Make sure you use different sizes for the different rope sizes. Block pulleys come in many different types — single, double, treble etc (see Fig. 65, C to F). I make all of mine these days but originally I bought them from the Danish firm Billings Boats (see Appendix 1 for address). They have small displays in some model shops and their products

are useful for the beginner who would otherwise be put off by having to make some of the more difficult pieces (see Fig. 66, A to D).

Another diversion while rigging can be davits and their tackle. The making of the ship's boats can also be attempted although again you can buy these but they will need dressing up a little to make them look real. If the ship's boats are to be covered with a protective tarpaulin then you simply need a solid block of wood shaped like a boat. Fine cord tied across the boat looks good and this type of presentation saves a few hours of carving out the boat's inside. I cheat a little nowadays and use a ball file on a flex drive from a bench motor for the inside carving.

At the bow end things can get a little complicated. Ships with high forecastles like naval frigates and raters mounted the bowsprit below forecastle deck. In our model we have made the space between forecastle deck and the main deck solid at the bow end (see Fig. 25, B). This makes a convenient solid into which we can fit our bowsprit after drilling at the correct angle.

By about the 1850s ships both naval and merchant tended to have the bowsprit canted with the butt between two or four upright bitts on deck level and visible. The two different ages are shown (see Fig. 67, A to P and Fig. 68, A to J). The various fittings in these illustrations need not be replicated as accurately. Wire, sheet metal strips and small pieces of hardwood can be dressed up to look true. Further techniques are shown later.

Hopefully, the plans that you should be working from will show you all rigging. Avoid any plans that do not. What they probably will not show you is what has been attempted in the illustrations within these pages. Get researching with other books on the subject. You will

Fig. 65.

**Different ways to fix
the lower shroud lines.**

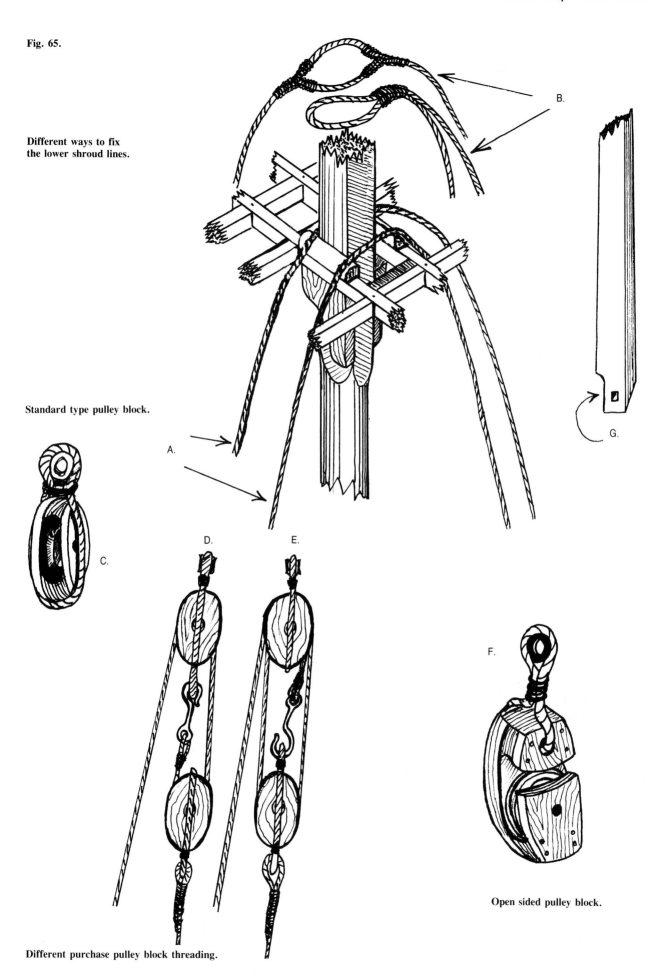

B.

Standard type pulley block.

A.

G.

C.

D.

E.

F.

Open sided pulley block.

Different purchase pulley block threading.

Fig. 66. Making pulley blocks.

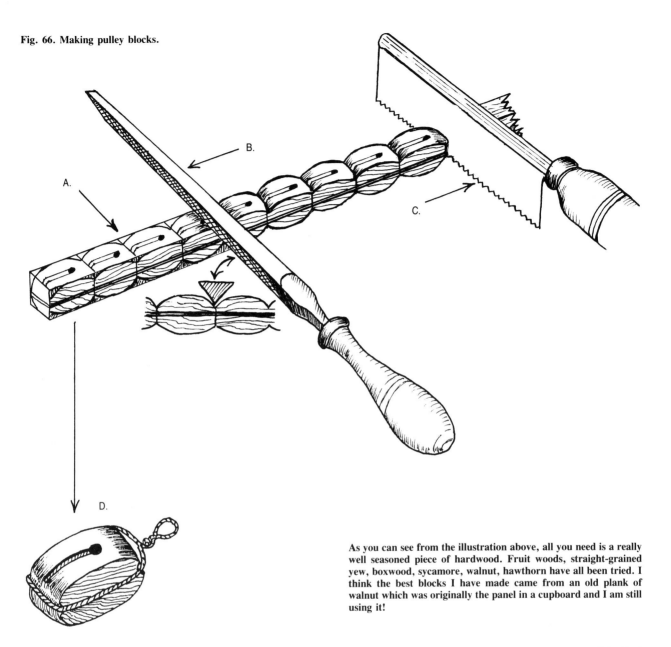

As you can see from the illustration above, all you need is a really well seasoned piece of hardwood. Fruit woods, straight-grained yew, boxwood, sycamore, walnut, hawthorn have all been tried. I think the best blocks I have made came from an old plank of walnut which was originally the panel in a cupboard and I am still using it!

Square up a length, making the cross-section measurement that of the block size. Mark off and drill a hole to simulate the throat of the block in each section. Use a 'V' file as illustrated. Groove each side for the sling rope. Cut each one and finish with sandpaper. Tie cord or use florist's wire around the block.

find that during the very long period that ships have been with us, man's ingenuity has come up with many different ways of solving the problems with sailing ships. Some ideas appeared and were then dropped only to reappear a century later with vast improvements. Iron fittings replaced the rather chunky wooden ones as refinements were made after the old 'Hearts of Oak' type ships began to disappear and were overtaken by the fast sailing ships from the 1780s onwards with their improved hull designs.

Useful tips

The good thing about making model ships is that the

volume of all the materials like wood, metal and cordage is quite low. A box of old scrap wire and offcuts of sheet metal can last you for years. Non-ferrous metals like brass and copper are the most useful and a couple of reels of florist's soft iron wire in two different gauges will last you for many a model. Try and build up a supply of these bits and pieces. Copper wire from high tension cables with individual wires that are thicker than normal are most useful. It is fairly soft and with a light hammer and a steel block as an anvil you can make a lot of fittings like chainplates and swivel trusses for main yards etc. (see Fig. 71, B to F, Fig. 72, C and Fig. 73, C). A later type of boom fitting is made from wire with beaten ends (see Fig. 71, F).

Fig. 67.

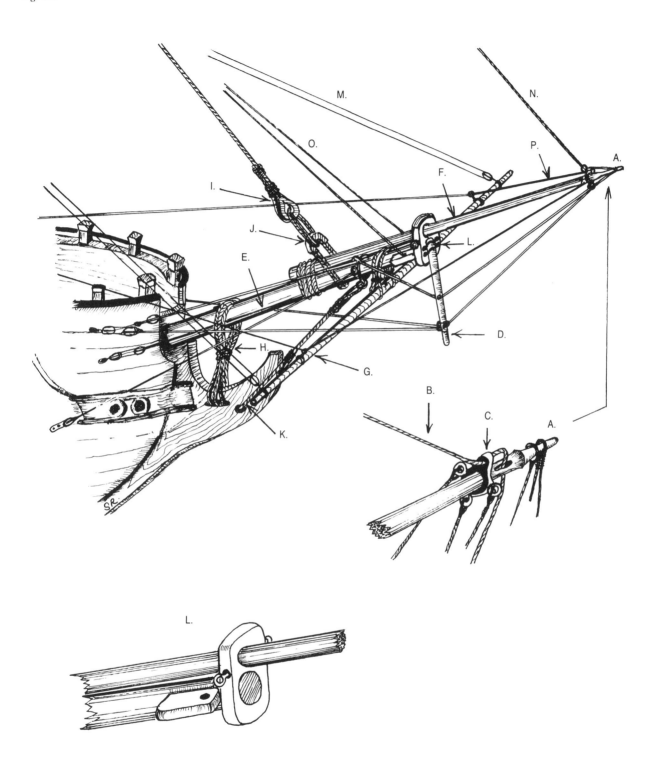

18th CENTURY

A. Jib boom tip
B. Jibstay
C. Traveller
D. Dolphin striker (martingale)
E. Bowsprit
F. Jib boom
G. Spritsail boom
H. Gammoning

I. Forestay & closed heart
J. Open heart
K. Bobstay
L. Bowsprit cap
M. Spritsail braces
N. Jibstay
O. Topmast stay & spring
P. Spritsail guys

The British packet ship *Rapid*.

Built 1833 at Shoreham, Sussex. Solid carved hull. These pictures have been included because the model was made without a plan. A few old prints and a painting were used as a reference, together with a little research. This is not the best way to do things but it was fun trying to get it right.

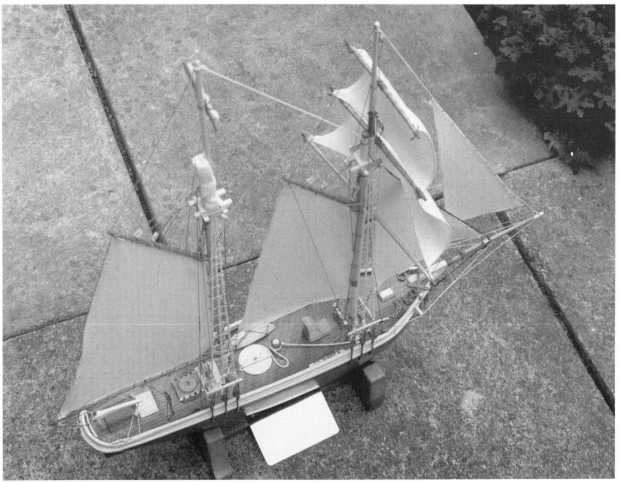

Fig. 68.

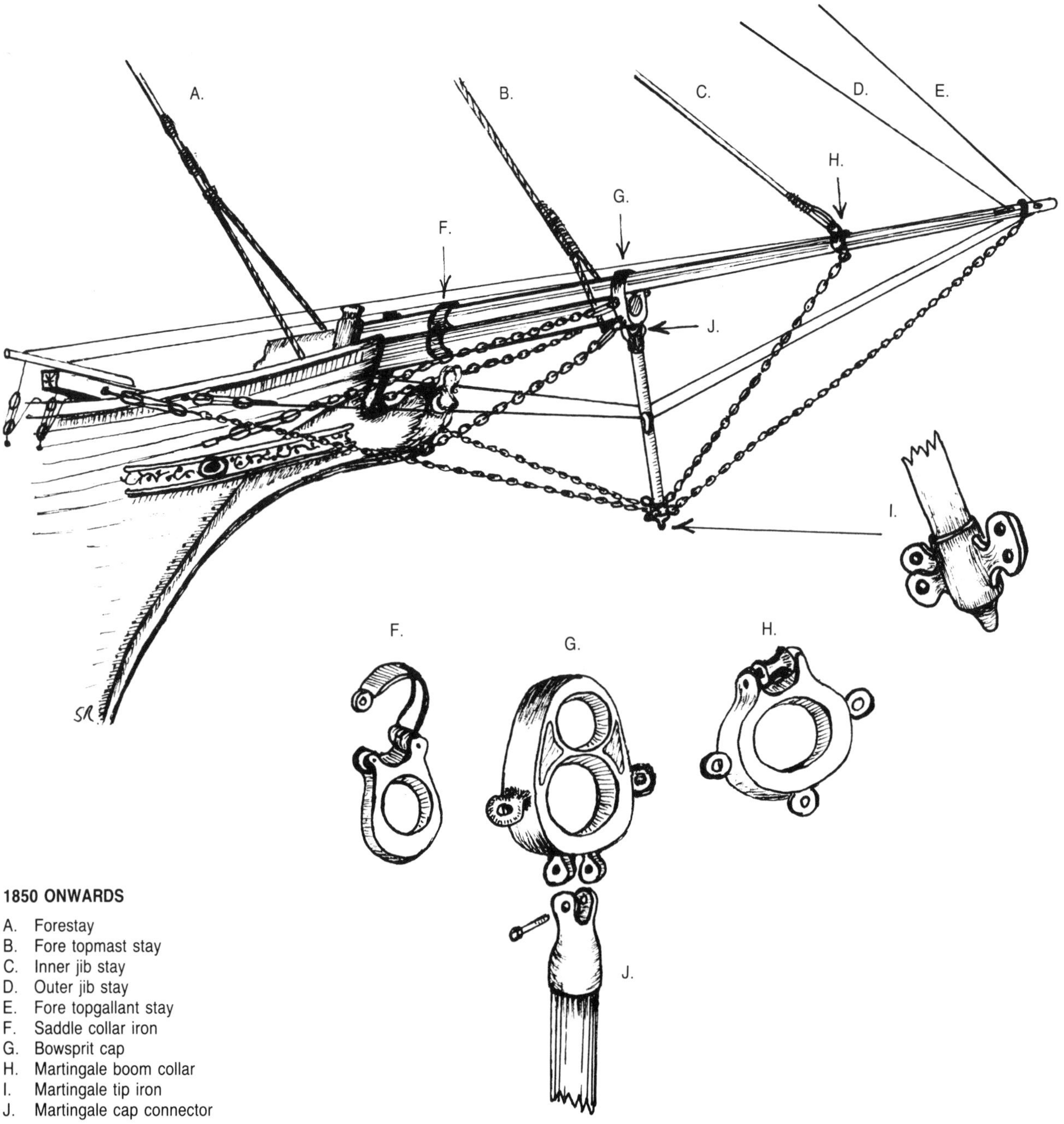

1850 ONWARDS

A. Forestay
B. Fore topmast stay
C. Inner jib stay
D. Outer jib stay
E. Fore topgallant stay
F. Saddle collar iron
G. Bowsprit cap
H. Martingale boom collar
I. Martingale tip iron
J. Martingale cap connector

Thin sheet metal like copper or shim brass will make mast caps (see Fig. 71, A). Use two pieces of wood the same size as your masts and wrap the metal, after thorough cleaning and tinning, around the pieces of wood in the manner shown. Use plenty of resin core solder around the outside. If this tends to spring undone use a small twist of oiled florist wire around the piece while soldering. You can drop some more melted lead into any spaces left. Clean off with a file and emery cloth ready for painting. Push out your wooden gauges. If you are good with working metals use a billet of $^3/_{16}$″ copper and make a solid mast cap by drilling and filing. I have made them from ebony or other very hard offcuts

of wood.

Metal bands, and there are many, can be a mixture of metal made ones and brown gummed sticky paper. Cut strips of this to the width of the band, dampen well and tightly wrap around the spar. Build up to the correct thickness and when dry paint carefully with matt black paint. You really will not be able to tell the difference from the metal type (see Fig. 73, A). Save any small tube offcuts, even old telescopic radio aerials, to cut off small pieces for metal bands (see Fig. 73, D).

Another difficult fitting is the stuntsail or stuns'l boom tip and rings. I cheat here on the smaller models — when the yard is ready to receive this fitting, drill into the end,

Fig. 71.

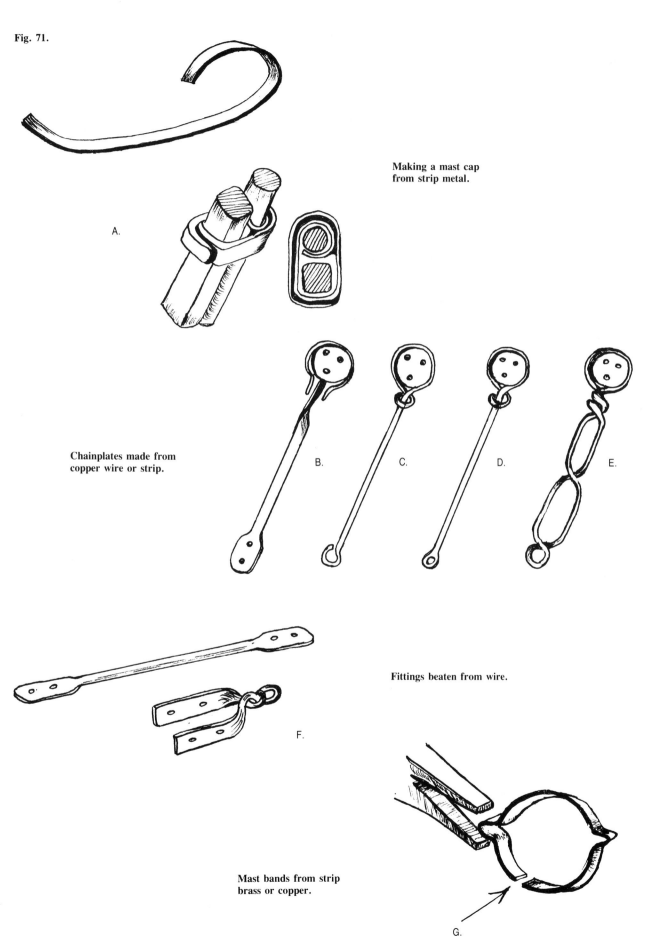

Making a mast cap
from strip metal.

A.

Chainplates made from
copper wire or strip.

B.

C.

D.

E.

Fittings beaten from wire.

F.

Mast bands from strip
brass or copper.

G.

(Note: there are no Figs. 69 & 70)

The *Rose Dorothea* 1906, Gloucester fisherman.

One of the many Grand Banks fishing schooners known for their speed.
This schooner was the first winner of the Sir Thomas Lipton trophy raced off Boston Harbour in 1907. She was built in 1906 in Provincetown.
Sailing boats of this type eventually developed into fast racing boats forming the basis of design for the modern racing yacht.
This model was carved from the solid and proved quite difficult to make in my small workshop, being something over three feet long. Note the four fishing Dorys each side of the waist deck nesting in one another.

then push in a brass nail or length of thick copper wire. Bend at right angles. The other boom support is another nail or piece of copper wire pushed into the yard further in from the tip. If you are making the stuns'l boom from a metal rod then this can be simply soldered onto the top of each of these metal projections. Dress the boom up a little with painted bands. If the boom is to be wood, then stick it on with Araldite. When all this is finished it is very convincing (see Fig. 72, A & B).

Mast collar bands are best made from sheet metal strips (see Fig. 71, G). They can be slipped onto the mast before fitting it to the hull but I usually make the band and solder the join when it is on the standing mast. The two crimps as shown in the illustration make two lugs and can be drilled to give various attachments to the collar.

Chainplates can be made from thickish copper wire (see Fig. 71, C to E). If you have notched these positions into the channel boards then you can twist the wire around the deadeye and make a small loop at the other end as C. You may choose to flatten the end tip and drill a small hole for fitting to the hull with a headed nail as D. In B, a strip of metal is used and twisted at the top. The deadeye has a wire bent around it and the two ends

soldered to the chainplate strip. In E wire is simply twisted. Use a dab of solder where they cross. Whichever method you use, fit the chainplates to the hull making sure they are seated in the notch. You can now add the wooden capping along the channel board edge.

Cannon balls, as already mentioned, can be shotgun pellets. A shot frame is simply made (see Fig. 73, E). Count out what numbers you need and in a tin lid coat with thin glue. Pile them into the frame and leave to set. Thin eggshell paint in black makes them look real.

Belaying pins are needed in plenty. I have tried making them from all sorts of things, but the best way is to nail small panel pins into a piece of scrap wood and carefully dip all the ends into old paint or emulsion. Keep the wooden holder horizontal, especially while they dry. If one dip is no good, do it again until you have the right shape. When these are thoroughly dry take them out of the wood carefully with small pliers and paint matt black (see Fig. 72, D). Araldite works well but is expensive.

A final piece of advice on metal. If you find your brass or copper a little too springy just anneal it by heating to red hot and quenching in water.

The finished model.

Fig. 72.

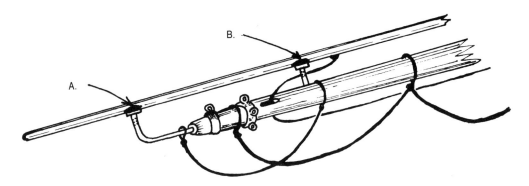

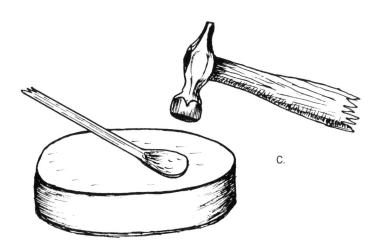

Stunt sail boom fittings.

Non-ferrous metals, like copper and brass. If annealed can be shaped on a steel block.

C.

D.

One method of making belaying pins.

Fig. 73.

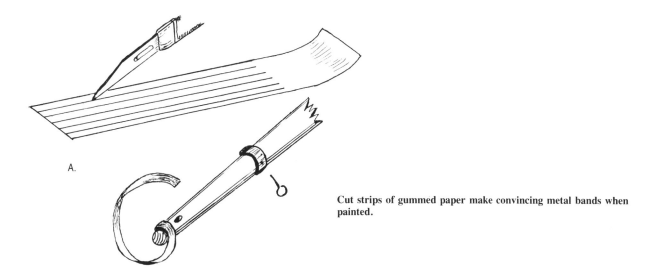

A.

Cut strips of gummed paper make convincing metal bands when painted.

Metal collar from strip copper.

B.

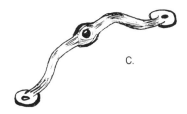

C.

Truss iron from thick copper wire beaten.

Old piping or radio aerials cut to make spar rings.

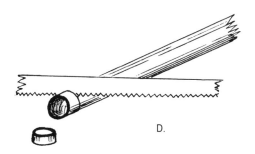

D.

Shot rack.

E.

93

The coastal barge *Emma* circa 1900.

This is a good one to begin modelling. The solid carved hull is not too difficult. It is a very solid looking job but these vessels had to be tough. Note the fore-peak sail is furled in this model. These vessels were sprit-rigged both on main mast and stern mizzen. There are plenty of photographs available of these old barges so detailing is easy for the beginner.

Fig. 74.

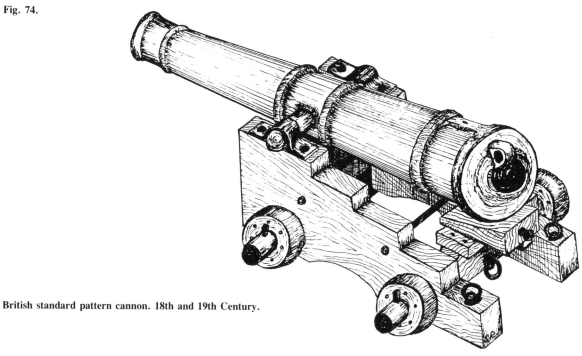

British standard pattern cannon. 18th and 19th Century.

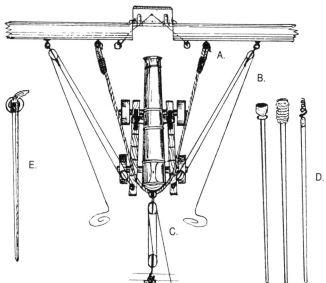

Plan of cannon breeching and tackle.

Gunport lids — three types.

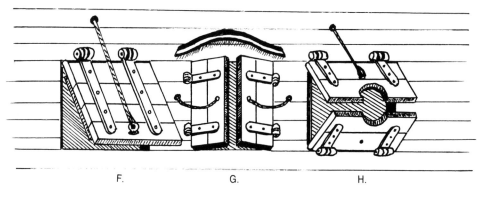

Armaments

The cannon was the main armament for attack and defence on naval ships and others like privateers, ships carrying letters of mark, and East Indiamen. They came in many different weights.

Guns changed very little after 1779 when the navy introduced the Carronade. This was a rather ungainly looking short, fat, gun made by the Carron Iron Foundry. It fired a relatively small charge but was loaded with a heavy shot and was used over short range. The navy called it a "smasher". The shot would explode on impact.

Later, around 1860, a new type of breech-loading gun was being developed but the general outline and gun carriage looked much the same as before.

The flint-lock was fitted to fire the gun, replacing the slow match around the 1770s and with the improvement of gunpowder, the length and size of some guns could be reduced.

In early times gun sizes were referred to by many fancy names. The largest gun firing a 50lb. ball was the original cannon. The demi-cannon with a 32lb. ball, the culverin with a 17lb. ball with barrels of different lengths, and the demi-culverin with a 9lb. ball. There were others, the saker, the minion, the falcon and falconet all played their part.

It was eventually more convenient to refer to the gun size and power by the weight of the iron balls they would throw, like 42, 36, 24, 18, 12 and 9 pounders. The heavier guns were mounted on the lowest decks to keep the ships trim at a safe balance. Cannonets were sometimes mounted on swivels to the main tops of warring ships and in the British Navy were controlled by the marines. Their effect was devastating when charged with multiple types of shot like cannister shot and used against the enemy decks when grappled alongside in close action.

Our interest in the deck guns for our model concentrates on a standard type on its gun carriage (see Fig. 74) and the way it is mounted and controlled on the deck. Similar carriages were used for the different weights of guns, they were simply made bigger and stronger for the larger varieties.

To move the gun and range it, or when loading and running out, needed tackle. Side tackle, train tackle and breeching ropes, together with pulley blocks, did all of this (see Fig. 74, A, B & C).

Ramrods for the charges and shot ramming, mops to dampen and clean the barrel after each firing and a worm for removing unfired charges were all part of the gun crew's equipment. A wheeled lever bar to slew the cannon when aiming should be included and adds authenticity to the gun deck areas if these can be included (see Fig. 74, D & E).

A lot will depend on the size and scale of your model. Simple simulations of gun carriages can be made to look very convincing. Small pieces of wooden dowel can be tapered and carved for gun barrels. Matt black paint gives the look of solid metal. You can of course buy model gun barrels of the period from model shops. These are lathe-turned in brass and are very expensive. Ask your local gun shop for a selection of different weights of shotgun pellets. These little lead balls make excellent cannon balls! (No. 5 shot for ⅛th scale 32 pounders.)

Gunport lids

These are usually marked on plans as just a row of small squares so some information on gunport types is worth a mention.

Gunports were usually double hinged along the top edge. Some opened like double doors and had a pair of hinges on each side. Another variety also had double flaps but hinged top and bottom. Some ships dispensed with lids altogether on their quarterdecks as at this level the ports were well clear of the water and the guns were in the open anyway. Brigs, corvettes, sloops and small schooners had small rowing ports between the gunports for the large sweep oars to be used when the ship was becalmed. Sighting holes and air vent flaps were sometimes incorporated in lids.

The port lids were raised or opened by a rope attached to the outside of the lid (see Fig. 74, F to H). The rope was threaded through a small hole in the bulwark called a bee hole. It was then tied off on a ring attached to a beam. On some ships the port lids had spray water deflectors like eyebrows over each port called rigols. This stopped water dribbling down over the port when in use (see Fig. 74, G).

In heavy weather the lower decks gunports were shut tight and caulked as they sometimes dipped into the water when the ship heeled heavily in a storm.

Apart from the standard cannon, already described, there are three other types of armament that are of interest to the model maker.

Mortar (A)

The illustration shows a 64 pounder. These were mounted on a solid wooden bed. The trunnions projecting from the base end of the mortar are kept in place by two stout metal saddles bolted down to the wooden bed. Each end of the mortar bed has a hoisting and lashing ringbolt. A wooden wedge quoin is used to fix the elevation.

These guns were used on bomb vessels or bomb ketches especially reinforced for this type of artillery and used for bombarding towns and installations on land. The angle of fire for this type of gun was approximately 45°. In some instances the ship could lob the shot over a headland and so avoid the enemy and its artillery after anchoring with care out of sight. The shot was hollow in most cases, filled with powder and fused to explode on contact shortly after.

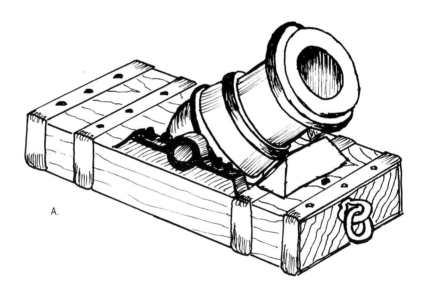

A.

Swivel pivot guns (B)

These small guns could change their direction of fire much quicker than the heavy deck gun. This was particularly useful when alongside the enemy. The piece was mounted on a pivoted swivel at various points and usually charged with multiple shot. Guarding enemy prisoners on deck after capture was another use found for this short range gun. Usually made of brass or bronze it had a protruding iron handle for control and could be depressed to fire into raiding party boats or if mounted on the tops, down on enemy decks. This gun was sometimes mounted on the larger type of ship's boat when used away from the main warship.

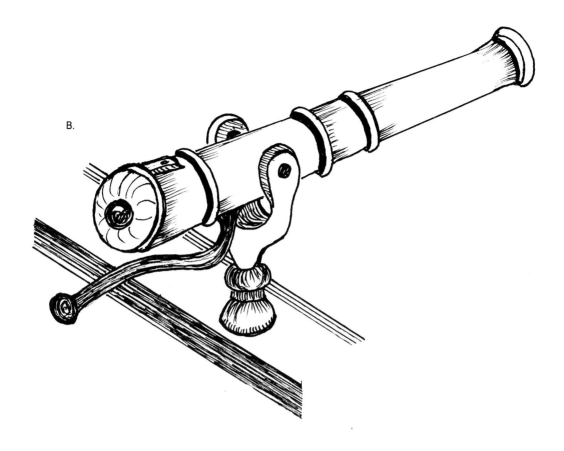

B.

Carronade (C)

A short, heavily built carriage gun developed in this country and favoured by the Royal Navy during the French wars. This was used as an auxiliary to the main armament over relatively short distances. The gun was loaded with a small charge but fired a heavy shot. The illustration shows the deck position after firing and when ready for reloading. This particular carriage is in two sections. A sliding mount on the truck takes the recoil on firing. When loaded the tackle pulls the barrel forward for sighting and firing. A worm thread fixed to the rear of the barrel replaced the quoin wedge used for many years to sight naval guns.

C.

Tools you will need

Necessary tools:

1. Standard wood saw
2. Fret or coping saw
3. Files, various including rasp plane
4. Bead or fine dovetail saw
5. Stanley knife or similar
6. Scalpel knife with replaceable blades
7. Medium or small ball pane hammer
8. Small or jeweller's hammer
9. Fine round-nose pliers (jeweller's type)
10. Ordinary pliers and screwdrivers
11. Medium size tin snips or heavy scissors
12. Small hand drill (model maker's electric is best)
13. Smooth iron block as anvil
14. Small bench-mounted vice or, better still, model maker's vice
15. Bulldog clips, ordinary spring pegs etc.
16. Small block plane
17. Various home-made scrapers
18. Chisels — ⅛", ¼" and ½"
19. A model maker's thumb plane
20. A soldering iron, small variety
21. Two pairs of tweezers

Some tools that make life a little easier:

1. Fine bandsaw or fret-saw, motor driven
2. Flex drive driven chuck, motor driven
3. Small lathe, home-made or otherwise
4. Model maker's soldering iron
5. Model maker's small circular saw
6. Model maker's pillar drill, electric
7. Large bench wood vice and model maker's G cramps

If you choose to buy fittings from the model shop you can dispense with a number of tools on the list. It is up to you and your pocket.

There are so many different types of historic craft which you can make from the most primitive fishing boat to the complicated naval vessels of the 1700s onwards, so start simple and work your way through to the more detailed varieties. Each ship is interesting, however humble. They were all designed or simply evolved to fill a need. I have made very convincing model ships where no plans ever existed. The more you read about ships the easier it becomes, so have a go!

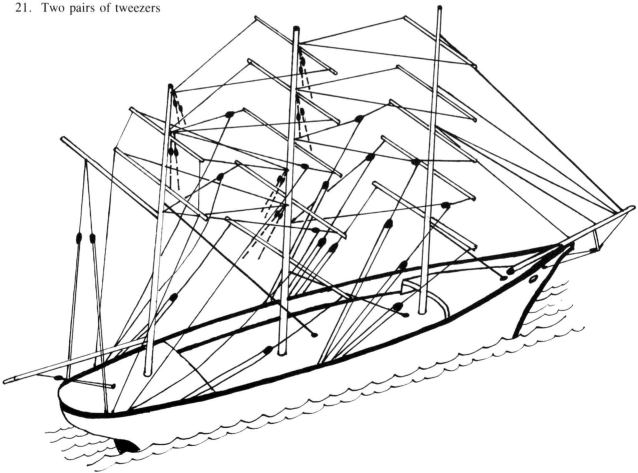

Fig. 75a.

A fast sailing ship of the 1850s.
Some of the major running rigging showing the use of pulley blocks that control the bracing of yards and booms.

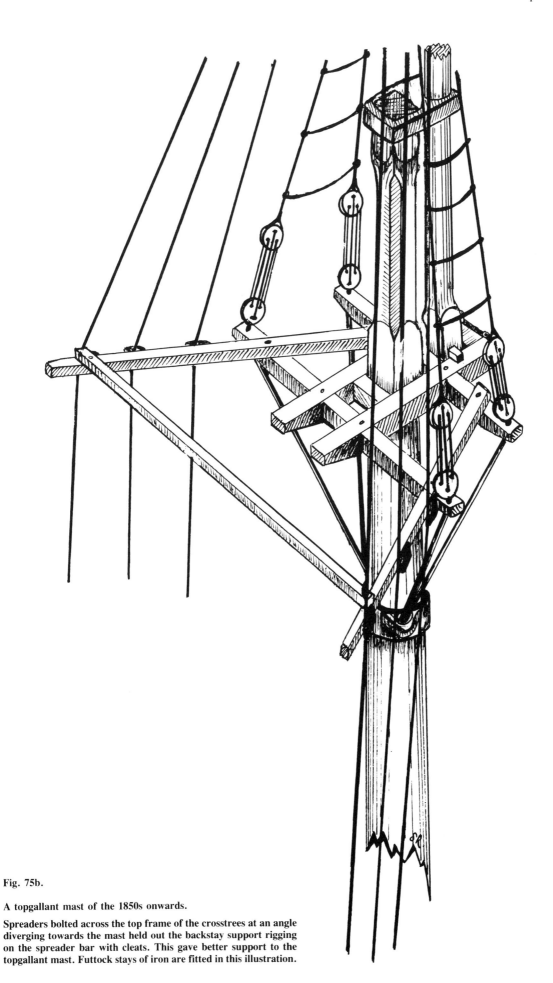

Fig. 75b.

A topgallant mast of the 1850s onwards.

Spreaders bolted across the top frame of the crosstrees at an angle diverging towards the mast held out the backstay support rigging on the spreader bar with cleats. This gave better support to the topgallant mast. Futtock stays of iron are fitted in this illustration.

101

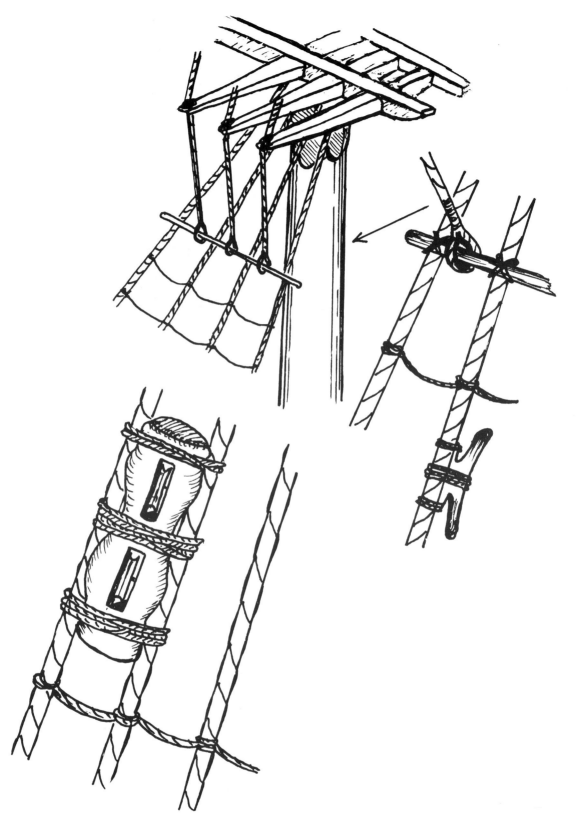

Futtock ropes, under the tops, are fixed to a bar lashed to the shrouds. These futtock ropes may be of iron in which case they are joined to a mast collar and are called futtock stays. The shrouds often had belaying cleats of hardwood lashed to them in appropriate places. Sister blocks containing one or more pulleys were also lashed to rigging shrouds for lifts and to control top gear.

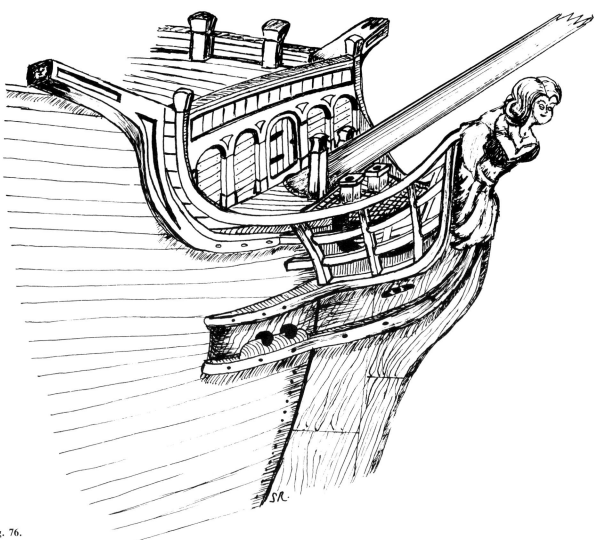

Fig. 76.

The beak head of a large ship of the 1780s.

Avoid this kind of model until you feel more confident or like a real challenge.

Simple sail making

Making a set of sails for your model boat is really a matter of taste. Of all the models I have attempted and completed only about thirty per cent have had sails.

You will see that this is so with models in museums or in model ship publications, whether old or contemporary models are shown. Badly made or ill-fitting sails can spoil an otherwise well-made model. Those really old and valuable shipwrights' models with their original sails can look very sad. The material is invariably rotten or badly discoloured unless the model is cased.

The sail, as a method of propulsion, has been around since about 6000 B.C. in some shape or form. On the kind of model ships we have discussed two basic types of sail are of interest, the square sail and the fore and aft type, usually found together on the same vessel. Remember that much of the loving detail on your model

will vanish partly behind the sails, if fitted, when viewed from a normal position.

The usual material used to make the sails on these historic ships was canvas of different weights. Some old ships carried a suit of strong cotton sails for use in light airs but these often suffered from mildew and rotted easily. Head sails like the main jibs were doubled to withstand the heavy wear.

We shall be trying to simulate canvas sails but will be using a different material. Modern canvas, however fine, is not suitable. It is all a question of scale of the weave and its flexibility.

The bolts of canvas were not very wide in their weave so the lengths had to be seamed together along the selvedges as these were a lot stronger than a cut edge. The canvas was not always used in a straight fashion. Some sails had to be shaped with gores (cut on the cross) to give the correct aerodynamic curve to the sail, like the bunt or belly of a square sail. This applied more to topsails which were cut full to make a bag form to collect as much air as possible. Main courses on square riggers had no, or very little, bunt shaping. Our model sets of sails will not need to have this kind of cutting procedure unless of course you want to try your hand at this.

I have tried three or four different types of cotton materials, including best pocket handkerchiefs, to make sails from. A dirty cream colour looks better. Some trading and fishing vessels had tan coloured sails. Look for some unbleached materials like fine calico. The weave should be as fine as possible. You could look at the bleached type. The very finest linen, if you can get it, will make fine sails.

Never make the sails until the model is finished or nearly finished. Using a ruler, some scissors and a few clips we shall make a template sail from paper. This is a trial and error process that I find safer than relying on the sail plans supplied with the model ship plans. With the latter everything will work using the plan providing you have got the model exactly right to the nearest

millimetre with all the yard exactly spaced etc. By all means follow your sail plan for the general shape of sails.

When you have cut your first paper square sail (see Fig. 77, A) clip the head of the sail to its yard and see if it is full enough to give a nice curve when the clews are touching the lower yard.

For the fore and aft sails like the mizzen spanker you can follow a similar procedure on all of its four sides, making sure the shape you have cut fits exactly the space between mast gaff and boom, no more and no less. The jib and stay sails are also treated in the same way regarding the space they occupy.

When all the paper sails are cut and trimmed to your satisfaction lay them on your carefully pressed material. Each sail will have to be with the weave direction correctly placed (see Fig. 77, A & B and Fig. 78, C, D & E). Use the lines drawn across the sail outlines in the illustration for the run of the weave.

Hold or weight the paper template and with a soft pencil draw a line around the outside edge of the template along the material. This will give you the exact sail size

The Topsail schooner *My Lady* circa 1890 is a pretty ship. There were many of these small schooners about in the 1860s onwards and many could still be found in use in the early 1900s. A few of them ended up being used privately by boat enthusiasts and weekend sailors in the 1920s.

Fig. 77.

Square sail.

Mizzen spanker.

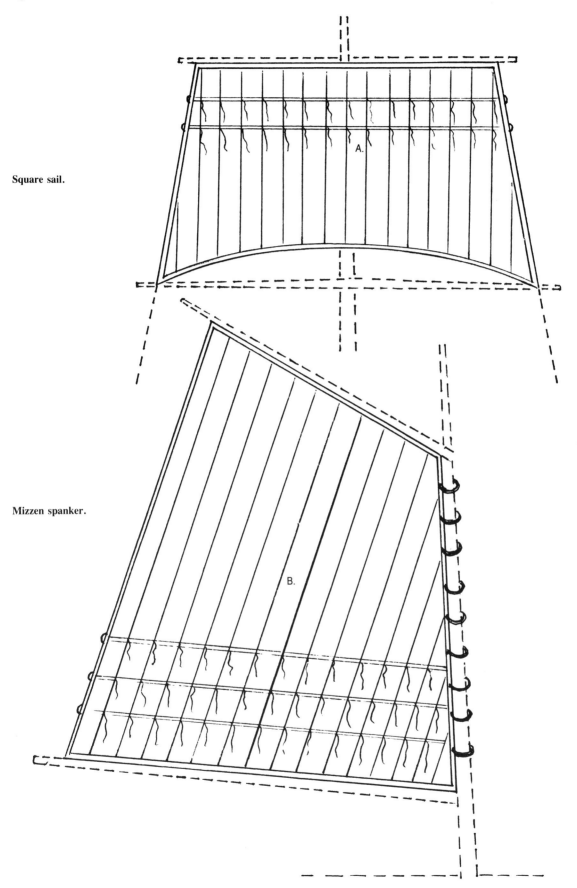

A.

B.

Fig. 77 *continued.*

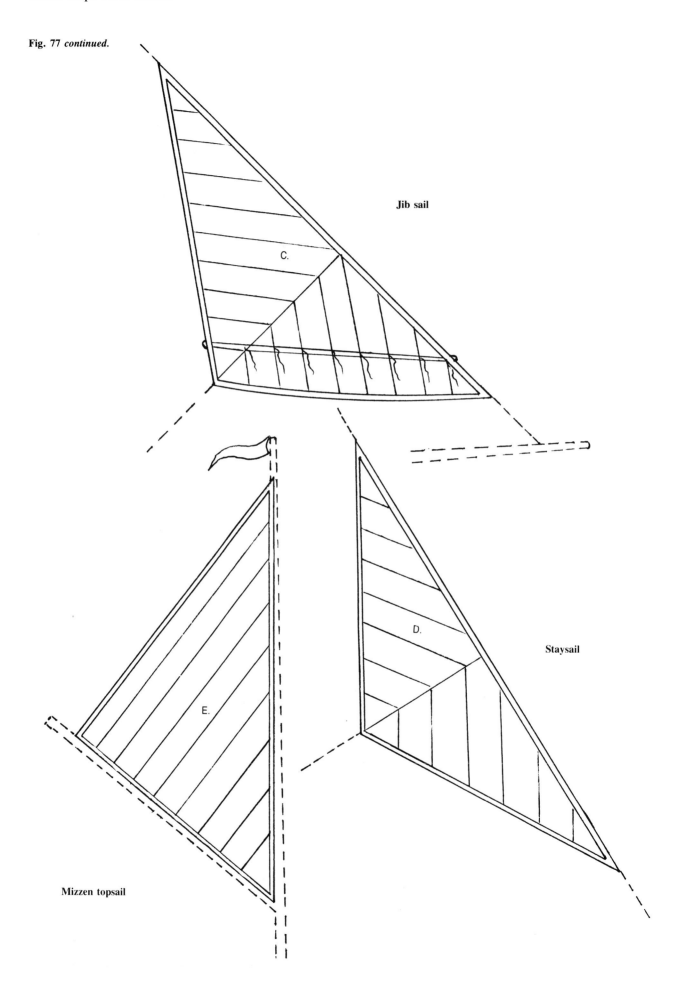

Jib sail

C.

D.

Staysail

E.

Mizzen topsail

Fig. 78. The deck layout of a typical top sail schooner circa 1890.

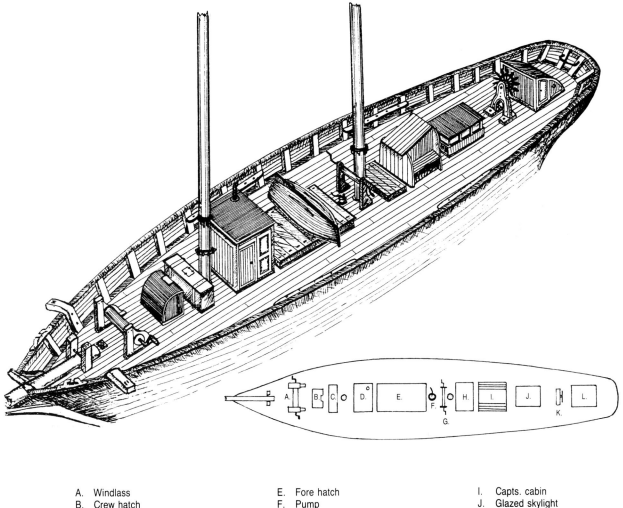

A. Windlass	E. Fore hatch	I. Capts. cabin
B. Crew hatch	F. Pump	J. Glazed skylight
C. Water tank	G. Winch	K. Ship's wheel
D. Galley	H. After hatch	L. Rope locker

marked on the material. Remove the template and draw with a ruler another line on the outside of the first line — about ⅜″ away. This is the cutting line. Cut out the sail. The regular use of a medium heat iron is indispensable from now on. Along the inner line fold over carefully (see Fig. 79, A) and press along the fold line. Do the same all around the sail whether three or four sided.

This is now the time to get the sewing machine threaded up with cotton of the same colour as the sail material, or perhaps a cotton slightly darker. Sew around the sail. The run of stitches should be a constant ⅛″ inside the fold edge (see Fig. 79, B). When you have been right around the sail trim off very carefully a sliver of material with sharp scissors so that the distance from the fold to the stitch line is ⅛″ and from the stitch line to the cut edge is also ⅛″. Press the sail well at this stage (see Fig. 79, C).

You can now put in rows of stitches evenly spaced across each sail to simulate the canvas joins on a real

sail. Press again very well. Follow the line diagram for direction of seams (see Fig. 77, A–D).

Reefing points can now be put on your sails. Three rows are normal on the spanker, two or three on a square sail and one or two on main jib sails. Run a row of stitches across the sail for this and with a threaded hand needle make the small lengths of reefing ropes both sides of the sail. I thread these through then cut them all the same length. With a needle or piece of wire dipped in thin glue dab a very small dot where the cotton or cord goes through the sail. When dry press with iron so that they all hang downwards on both sides.

A final note on finishing your sail sets. If you can find a very small eyelet set used for small belts in your local needlework shop, you could try eyeletting the sail corners. This would be suitable for the larger type of model sails. The eyelets come in different colours so go for black or grey. The kit comes with a small tool for pressing these into the material.

The steam yacht *Medea* 1904.

The *Medea* was launched at the Alexander Stephen's yard, Linthouse, Glasgow in 1904 and believe it or not is still going strong today at the San Diego Maritime Museum. A very pretty little steam yacht to make.
I cased my model as you can see from the photo also writing a short history that I mounted on a brass frame within the case.

The finished model cased, showing a brief history mounted in brass frame.

Aerial view taken through glass case.

Bow deck area.

Close-up of bridge area.

Fig. 79.

**Fold over along the inner
line all around edges.**

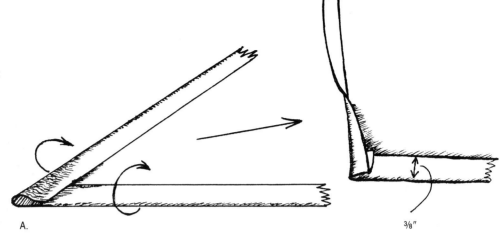

A.

3/8″

**Press well and stitch around edge.
Trim off ⅛″ sliver as described.**

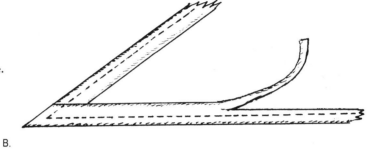

B.

Press the finished seams again carefully.

⅛″
⅛″

C.

Finished sail corner with rope fitted.

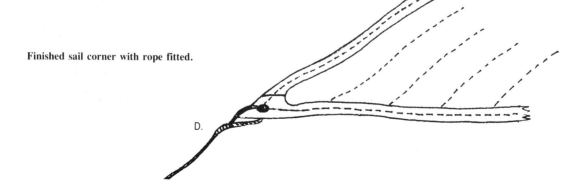

D.

Make sure you have pressed the sail very well. Keep the iron on the correct setting to avoid scorching! Rope sheet attachments can be fixed through the corners (see Fig. 79, D).

When lacing on the head of a square sail to its yard or the mizzen spanker to the gaff and boom use a threaded needle with plenty of spare thread or cord. Follow the system described (see Fig. 38, J). This is a continuous cord and can be tightened and then tied off when you come to the end of the spar.

Real sails have a bolt rope around their edges. On really large models you may wish to imitate this with suitably laid cordage. Catch stitch this to the edges of the sail. It is difficult but keep this in mind for the really large model.

Your sail plan may call for sail hoops to be fitted to the luff edge of the spanker sail. These join the edge of the sail to the lower mizzen mast. I usually make these from copper wire. Wrap the wire around a piece of dowel slightly larger than the mast's diameter. Cut through all the hoops and when they are all separate pierce the sail luff edge with a sharp gimlet and work the hoop through the hole and around the mast. Reshape if necessary with small long nose pliers. If the wire is too bright, colour with matt brown paint before you thread the hoops (see Fig. 77, B). This illustration shows sail hoops fitted.

The hoop attachment to the sail luff edge as described is the easy way to do this and applies to all luff edges including your three-sided sails. In reality these attachments are a little more complicated to achieve, especially on the smaller scale models.

The sail hoops were laced to the luff edge with stout lines, passing through the eyelets or cringles which were sewn onto the luff edge bolt rope. On the jib and staysail luffs the same applied except that the hoops were smaller rings. This enabled these sails to be free running when hoisted, the rings running up and down the different stay lines.

Mounting your model ship

The first requirement is a nice piece of timber for a base plaque. Perhaps an old drawer front or some other section of planking from old furniture. Failing this, a piece of hardwood timber from your local yard.

I have used quartered oak with a good fleck in the grain, also mahogany types and walnut. You need a plank no thinner than ⅞" thick. The plank does not have to be as long as the ship's hull. Try holding the model over the wood before finally cutting to your length. This will give you the best idea.

Try and get planed wood. Sand it to a nice smooth finish and bevel the edge. You could put on a fancy bevel if you have a routing machine but be careful that you can use it. I have ruined a few planks learning this technique. (See Fig. 80, A, B & C.)

Two different methods of mounting your ship are now possible. Vertical metal pillars can support the ship's hull which means that the ship is permanently fixed to its stand. In the second method we make a shaped cradle for the hull. The ship can be lifted off the stand at any time with this mounting (see Fig. 80, E).

For the first method any hollow rod of brass or bronze, shaped or otherwise, will do. I have used old brass cartridge cases and once a pair of miniature brass candlesticks bought at a boot sale. Model engineers have no problems here, they make them on their lathes.

Decide where the pillars will join with the ship's keel. Mark the keel. Measure between the two marks and transfer the two marks accurately onto a centre line of the board. Drill the board through vertically. Countersink the holes on the underside of the plaque slightly. The next part is tricky and involves drilling up into the keel of the model a little way — half an inch should be enough. Find two screws (thinnish ones) that will be long enough to pass up from the bottom of the board, through the pillars and into your model's keel. A small indentation filed into the top of the pillars may help the keel to settle nicely onto the pillars. Carefully tighten up the two screws. I have used this method many times. One small point — polish up the pillars before fitting.

The second method needs two pieces of flat timber of the same colour as the base plaque. They need to be approximately half the thickness of the plaque. Decide where the curved cradle sections are to support the hull and at these points make a rough template from card. You could use the same templates you have already used on the hull when making it. Any method of joining the two cradles to the plaque can be used. Be careful to look at the wood grain of the two cradle pieces before cutting out the shape of the hull (see Fig. 80, E). The grain should run vertically to the plaque.

A small strip of velvet ribbon on the inside curve of the two cradles can be added to finish off the stand.

The wood finish on your mount is up to you. Mild stain then wax polish or a light varnish may suit your taste. I always like the contrast between a nicely waxed plinth and polished brass pillars, it looks more professional.

Name plates for your model mount

You will want to finish off your model plinth with a suitable name plate. I find the best metal for this is brass. Cut a small plate of the metal after making a paper template to size. Work out the number of words on the paper. I use a small electric vibro tool for the job of engraving. It is not as good as a professional hand engraver's work but it doesn't look too bad. Always drill and polish your metal plate before engraving.

If the above sounds too difficult then put the information into a little brass frame, the type sold for small photos. You can type or have set a potted history of the ship and fix the frame at an angle on the plinth. This can look very professional and finishes off the whole project. (see top photo page 108).

111

Fig. 80.

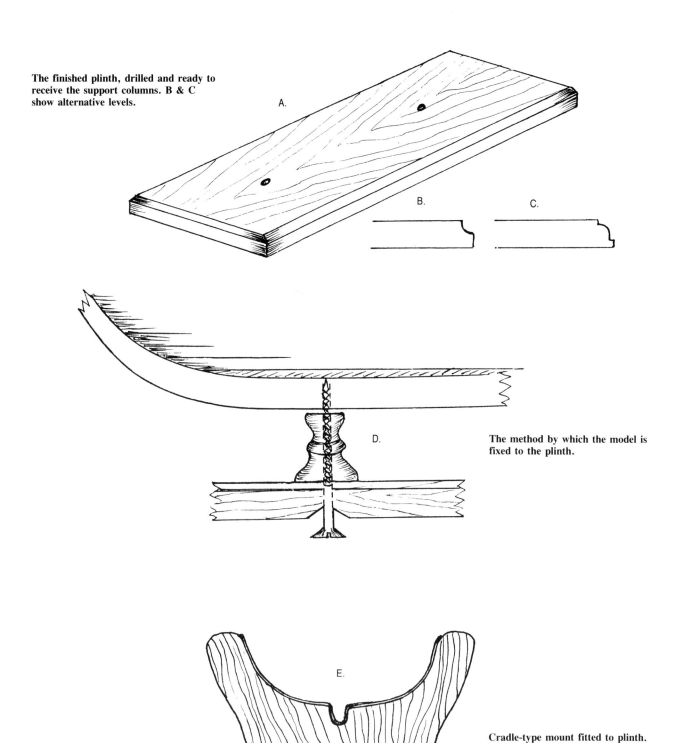

The finished plinth, drilled and ready to receive the support columns. B & C show alternative levels.

A.

B.

C.

D.

The method by which the model is fixed to the plinth.

E.

Cradle-type mount fitted to plinth.

Fig. 81

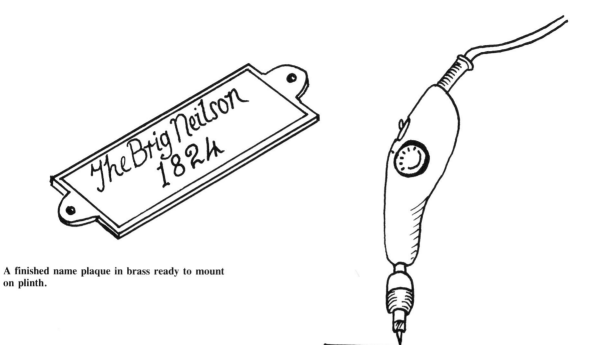

A finished name plaque in brass ready to mount
on plinth.

A vibro engraving tool will need getting used to.
Not as good as real hand engraving however.

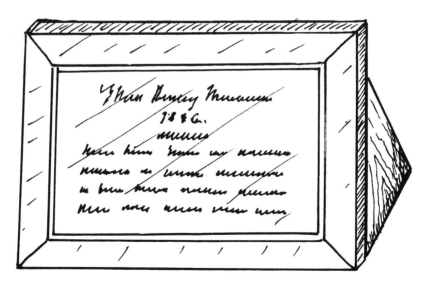

Use a small brass photo frame to hold the historical details of your
model and mount on the stand (see top photo on page 108).

The finished model of *Alabama*.

HMS frigate *Raleigh* **1776. Ex American Navy.**

The *Nina*, one of the fleet of three ships including the *Santa Maria* that set sail in August 1492 for America. The *Santa Maria* never returned but Columbus came back to Europe in the *Nina*, his favourite ship, we are told.
There were no plans available for this little ship but the National Geographic magazine had some very good perspective drawings — the rest was researched.

Sailing barges

No other wooden sailing vessel in Great Britain has survived for so long into this century. The barge is probably one of the strongest hull forms ever evolved, its shape and the gear of these sturdy craft seem to belong to a different family altogether from other sailing boats we have discussed so far.

Somebody once said that everything about a barge was practical before it was beautiful and it was beautiful because it was right, so they are worthy of a special mention here.

A barge is a good model to start with and a first-time carver will not be over-taxed in finding the right shape from his block of wood, the shape lends itself to solid carving. Sailing barges as we know them developed from a box-like craft, flat bottomed and used on rivers and estuaries in the 18th century. These early load carriers, not unlike latter day lighters, were entirely open craft. It was not until 1810 that decking and large hatch openings appeared.

By 1840 the wedge-shaped swimhead bow was superseded by the straight stem. The transom stern was developed after 1860 and these vessels began to look very much like those occasionally seen today, owned by enthusiasts and clubs.

Sailing matches in the 1860s developed a need and gave incentives for the development of faster hull shapes and by the mid 1890s these new craft were being used well beyond just river and estuary limits.

The main building centres were in the south-east coastal areas of England. Places like Ipswich, Harwich, Malden and Rochester were some of the coastal towns where building yards flourished and coastal trading took place. The Rivers Thames and Medway were also important barge building areas. Coastal barges traded across the North Sea to Europe and as late as the 1930s large schooner-rigged barges went as far afield as British Guyana in South America.

They came in all sizes. Big coastal sea-going barges had wide decks and small hatches for safety's sake. In safer waterways the river and estuary barge had a narrower beam but larger hatches, making cargo handling an easier task. Hatch coamings were usually 12 inches high on river barges but up to 24 inches on the larger sea-going barges. These differences and others help in recognising the various types of barges when considering the vessel to make as a model. Old photographs can be of immense help when researching for deck detailing.

Barge-type vessels used various sail plans, but the economical main spritsail with a mizzen mast sail which was either mule-rigged or sprit-rigged was favourite. Crews for this type of rig could be reduced to the bare minimum. A captain and mate was usual with perhaps an extra hand or more when sea trips were undertaken around the coastal areas.

The model maker will find a number of different types of winches, windlasses, dolly winches and crab winches on the barge deck so look out for these on the plans.

Plans for barges can sometimes be difficult to come by. It is rare to find any two barges of exactly the same in every detail because plans were rarely drawn. The foreman shipwright would take off all his measurements from a half model — that was the general practice — the rest depended on the eye of the craftsmen.

Plans Handbook No. 2 (published by Argus Specialist Publications) lists some plans and looking further afield there are some interesting Dutch barges to be considered.

The drawings in this book cannot show every detail on barges but will give first-time model makers a fair idea about these interesting craft, some of which still survive today. If you live near the water or can make a special visit to see one of these old craft, take a camera and notebook, you won't be sorry.

The following details list six different barge types:

Thames coastal barge

A ruggedly built ship, larger than the Thames 'River' class. Built originally for working the east and south coastal areas of Britain, and Continental ports. Bowsprits were fitted to these craft, the average length was 25ft. This spar was made of pitch or Oregon pine. Approximate sizes 85ft × 19ft × 7ft draught, sprit rigged and with leeboards. Large main hatch, small fore hatch.

Thames river barge

Similar in general lines to the coastal barge but is slightly smaller and in some cases narrower by comparison. The mizzen mast and sail is smaller than the coastal barge and is carried further aft, the sheet rope being led to the rudder blade top. It has no bowsprit and the mast is usually in a tabernacle. The working ground was usually the Thames and Medway and adjacent coasts. Approximate sizes 80ft × 18ft × 6ft draught. Sprit rigged, it had leeboards, a large main hatch and a small fore hatch.

'Stumpy' barge

A smaller variety of the Medway and Thames sailing barge. It had a stout pole mast in a tabernacle but no topmast or bowsprit. Some 'Stumpys' had no mizzen mast. It was sprit rigged and used leeboards.

Humber keel

A flat-bottomed Yorkshire craft of about 100 tons. One single hatch occupying almost all of the deck space. Leeboards were fitted and the mast in a tabernacle carried a large square mainsail and topsail. An inland waterway craft. Approximate size 60ft × 15ft × 7ft draught.

Norfolk wherry

A Norfolk Broads cargo vessel. They were mostly clinker built, unlike the carvel-built barges of other areas. A false keel was usually part of the construction and was bolted to the hull to assist sailing. A heavy heel end weighted the mast which was set in a tabernacle. One long single hatch from stern to just abaft of the mast. Approximate size was 55ft × 16ft, shallow draughted.

Dutch barge

This is a general term and covers many variants. It was almost flat-bottomed and had many features found on British barges. They had leeboards and some were originally sprit rigged. Known sometimes as 'Boir' yachts they had a single stout mast and in the gaff rigged types the gaff was curved. Used for freight transport in coastal waters. Models of these craft can look very attractive.

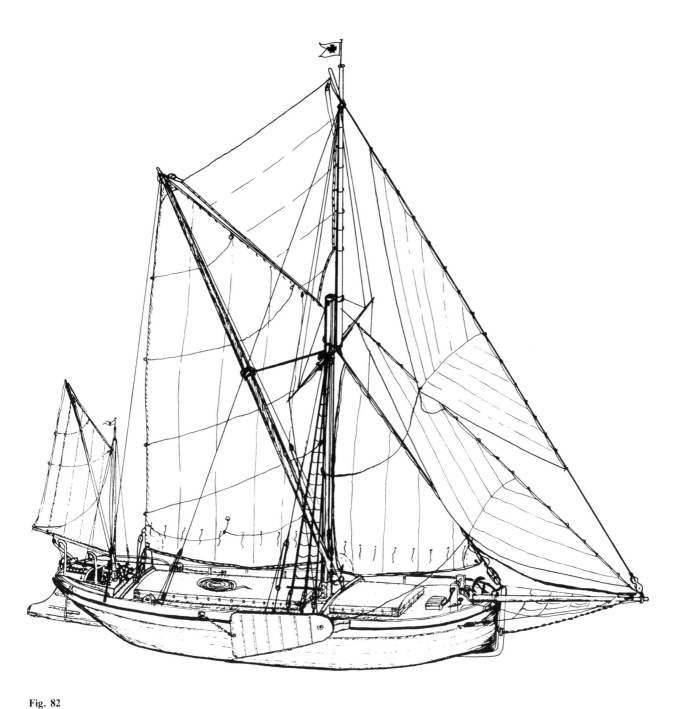

Fig. 82

Coastal sailing barge, circa 1900

A fully rigged coastal barge with sprit mainsail, mizzen, foresail, staysail, jib topsail and topsail rigged. In this illlustration the steering position is unprotected. Some barges had a small kiosk type wheelhouse with a separate hatchway to the small stern cabin that most craft had.

The British coastal barge *Charlotte* **circa 1900–1930**
The finished model.

The Catalan boat 1440.

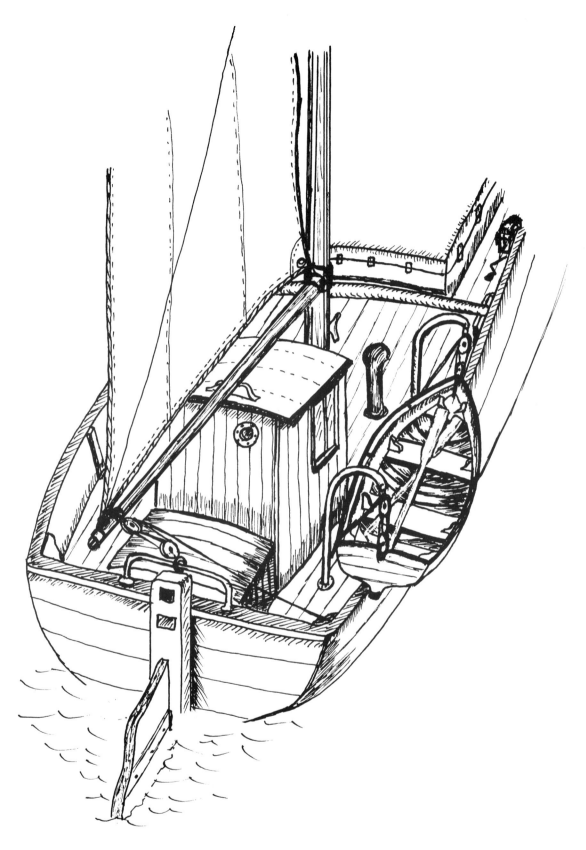

Fig. 83

Barge wheelhouse

The stern view of a barge wheelhouse sometimes fitted to seagoing coastal barges. There are probably more barges with unprotected steering positions, but you will find some plans which show a wheelhouse. When sailing barges were fitted with an auxiliary motor, wheelhouses were sometimes built. It is interesting to note that there was only one barge ever built with a motor. This was in the 1920s. Some barges had motors fitted well after they were built.

Steering gear can be either by chains and pulley or by a screw bar on a worm spindle with opposing threads. This is housed in a case under cover between stern and wheelhouse. The mizzen sheet traveller is connected to an iron horse on the top of the transom board.

Fig. 84

Barge bowsprit gear

Bowsprit detail found on sea going coastal barges. The gear supported the extra jib and jib topsail not present on river barges.

A. Long topmast stay
B. Bowsprit
C. Traveller ring
D. Inhaul rope
E. Outhaul chain
F. Bobstay to windlass
G. Shrouds
H. Gammon iron
I. Stayfall tackle

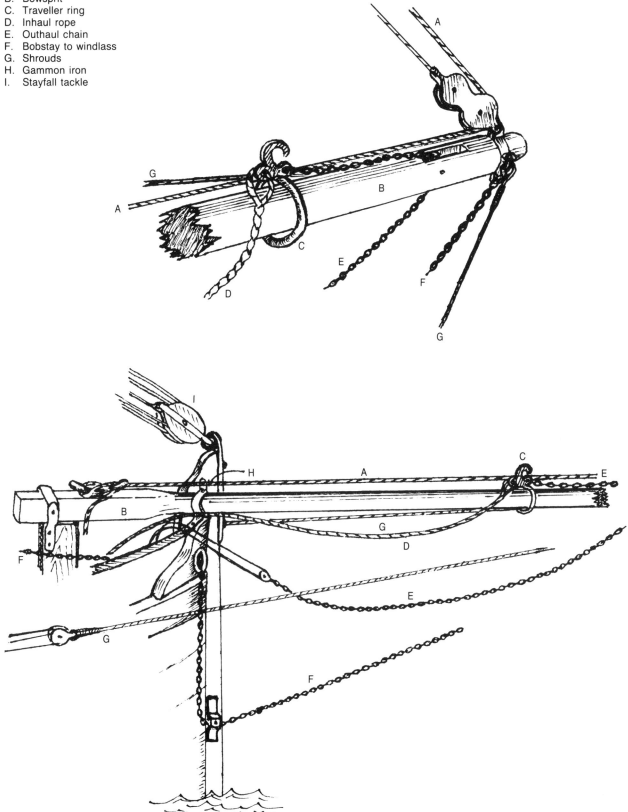

The squared-off butt end of the bowsprit was sometimes held firm in a bowsprit heel tabernacle.

Fig. 85

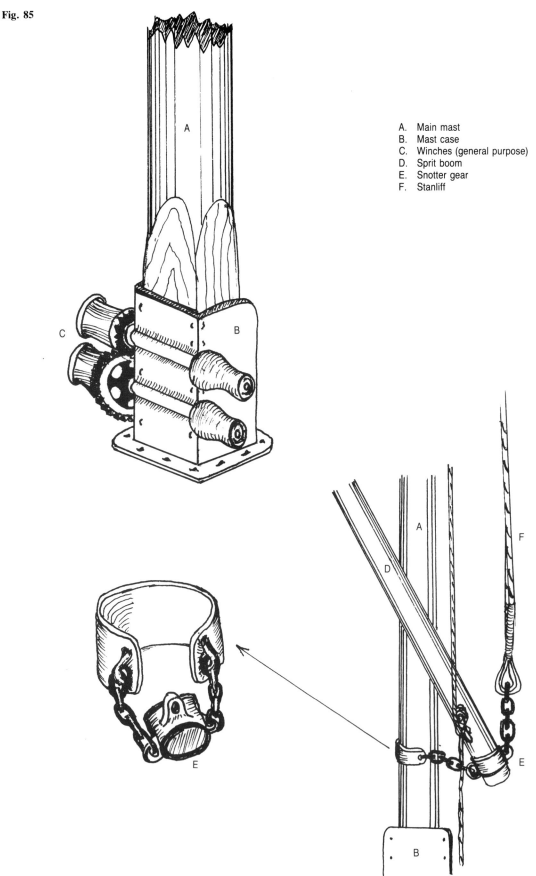

A. Main mast
B. Mast case
C. Winches (general purpose)
D. Sprit boom
E. Snotter gear
F. Stanliff

Barge main mast and sprit boom gear

The main mast case with general purpose winches. These were usually crank handled. The heel of the sprit boom has snotter gear with chain linking it to the mast. The sprit is always on the starboard side of the mast. Apart from supporting the main sprit boom heel with its enormous weight the gear kept the boom against the main mast.

Fig. 86

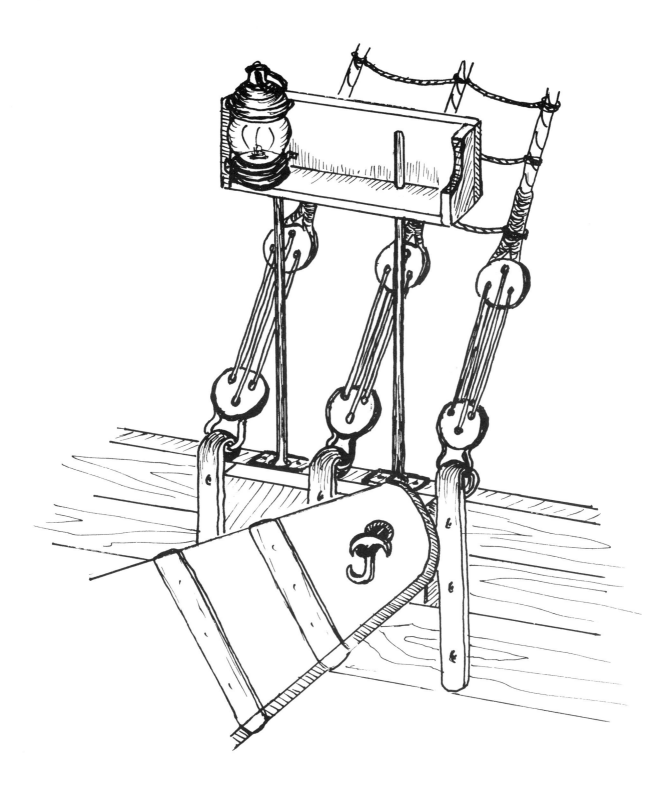

Light screen boxes

Light screen, a box-type holder for navigation lights, was usually lashed onto the main shrouds of sailing ships. Some barges, however, had screen boxes that were made to unship for the purpose of going alongside. Two iron rods with a forked top pierced the bottom of the box holding it up a few feet above the bulwark. The other end of the rods went into holes along the bulwark edge between the chainplates. Boxes, painted white, shielded the lights viewed from the stern so that at sea the light angle shone forward and to beam. A white stern light was usual.

Fig. 87

When considering the type of model ship to make try not to be too ambitious. The six illustrations would suit a beginner as they are interesting to make and not too difficult.

A. A dipping lugsail fishing boat. There were many working boats like this. Some had two masts like the Hastings lugger, warship galleys, Scottish fifies and skaffies.
B. The brig was a two-masted square rigged sailing ship with a single deck and a small poop deck. If you are impatient to make a square rigger, this is a good one to start with.
C. The topsail schooner was a very popular sailing ship in the 19th century, engaging in coastal trading in many places. Here you have a chance to make both square and fore and aft sails and rigging on the same project.
D. Schooners were fast yacht-like ships, rigged fore and aft. There are many variants of this ship to choose from. They include the famous Grand Banks fishing schooners and many other splendid American designed vessels.
E. The ketch was a popular rig among sailing trawlers. Brixham trawlers and some Lowestoft boats had this rig. A simple boat to start modelling.
F. The barge, as already discussed in detail, is a good model to start with. There are some plans for making actual sailing models of these vessels. Their shape and size can well accommodate any power source if fitted.

America has a formidable selection of historic ships. From Nova Scotia down the eastern seaboard to Florida Keys is where many interesting ships were built. The Delaware and Chesapeak Bay areas in particular simply reek of naval and maritime lore.

The Gloucester fishing schooner of 'Captain Courageous' fame, the Baltimore clipper schooner with its speed of sail engaged in many famous and infamous activities. Boat builders, as with the British cutter makers, usually laid two ships at once, one for the smugglers and one for the authorities to buy and chase them. The neat little Pinkys of New England and Massachusetts make good models. The list of types is endless. (See model photos of the above mentioned craft on pages 22, 74, 90 and 125).

The Baltimore clipper HMS *Mosquidobit* **Ex American Navy** *Lynx*.
Close-up view showing deck details.

The brig *Neilson*, built 1824

This photo illustrates what a hull looks like prior to the main planking job. The slightly higher poop deck, with its timber heads, was included into the bulkhead frames instead of making this deck separate from solid timber.

The poop cabin windows are not added yet in this picture. These bulge out over the stern on either side and are shaped from the solid then glued onto the hull. The window detailing is added later, using the same method as described on pages 60 & 61 for deck skylights.

The original Brig was built in 1824 by Edward Adams at Buckler's Hard, Hampshire, England, where many other famous ships were built.

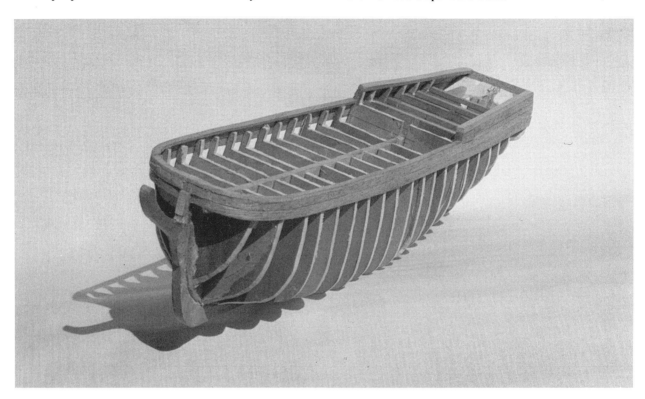

The finished hull frame from the bows before planking.

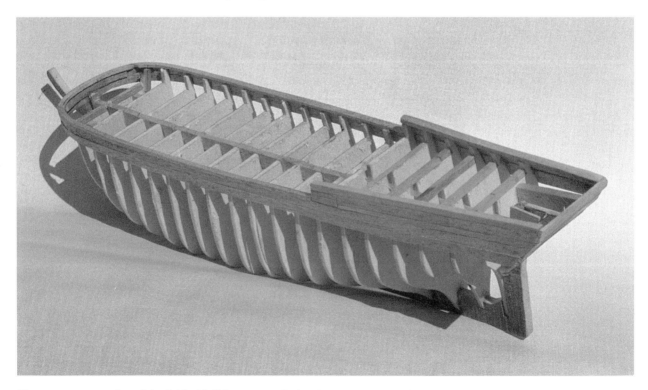

Three quarter stern view of the finished hull frame — ready for planking.

This picture of the brig *Neilson* shows the hull after planking with some of the deck detailing completed.

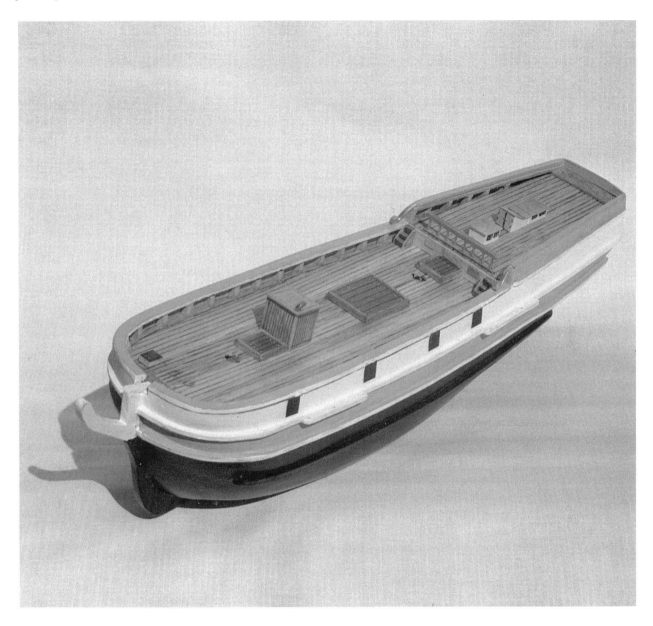

The following seven photos illustrate the completed brig *Neilson* from various angles.

The finished model mounted on a mahogany board. Note the brass uprights, made from 303 cartridge cases to support the model.

Actual hull length 19″
Overall length from tip of jib boom to stern davits 26″

The brig *Neilson* 1824.

A good example of a trading Brig. These were being built in the early years of the 19th century until about 1855. The *Neilson* was built at Buckler's Hard, Hampshire in 1824. She made a record passage in 1827 between Deal and Trinidad taking 44 days from 15th September to 29th October. Length 91′4″, beam breadth 24′2″. Depth of cargo holds 16′2″. This is a good type of ship to make for the modeller who has already made one or two successful ships.

A three quarter prow view of the finished model.

The sides of the brig. The hull planking was well filled and sanded to loose the grooves between the planks for this finish.

Close up of bow section showing the large windlass.

Stern view showing deck detail. Only a small amount of gilding was necessary near the cabin windows. This was made from twisted wire and gilded with paint.

Another stern view showing the small ship's boat slung from curved one piece davits.

A closer view of the deck detail.

A final word

Some of the ideas referred to in this book to help the beginner get around many of the problems might upset the professional model shipwright. The idea from the very beginning is to get the model enthusiast and the 'do-it-yourselfer' into this fascinating hobby. Start with a simple ship and always do a little research. It is quite interesting what additional information is lying around in libraries, museums and nautical institutions.

You have read the book — now make the film.

Appendix 1

Useful Addresses

Maritime Models Greenwich
7 Nelson Road
Greenwich
London SE10 Tel: 081–858 5661

Model Shipwright
International Quarterly Magazine
Conway Maritime Press Ltd.
101 Fleet Street
London EC4Y 1DE Tel: 071–583 2412

Argus Specialist Publications (Plans Service)
Argus House
Boundary Way
Hemel Hempstead, Herts.
HP2 7ST Tel: 0442–66551

Billings Boats A/S
Gejsing
6640 Lunderskov
Denmark

National Maritime Museum
Romney Road
Greenwich
London SE10 9NF Tel: 081–858 4422

Appendix 2

Bibliography

Anderson, R. C.	*Seventeenth Century Rigging*	Model & Allied Publications 1972
Bougnet, Michael	*South Eastern Sail 1840–1940*	David & Charles 1972
Campbell, G. F. M.R.I.N.A.	*Jackstay*	Model Shipways Co. Inc. N.J.
Chapelle, H. I.	*The Search For Speed Under Sail*	Geo. Allen & Unwin Ltd.
Chapman, F. H.	*Architectura Navalis Mercatoria*	Adlard Coles Ltd. 1768
Cooper, F. S.	*Handbook of Sailing Barges*	Adlard Coles Ltd. & John de Graff, N.Y.
Culver, Harry B.	*Contemporary Scale Models of Vessels of the Seventeenth Century*	Payson & Clarke N.Y. 1926
Davis, C. G.	*American Sailing Ships (Their Plans and History)*	Dover Pub. Ltd. N.Y.
Dudszus, Alfred & Henriot, Ernest	*Dictionary of Ship Types*	Conway Maritime Press 1986
Frere-Cook Gervis (Ed)	*The Decorative Arts of the Mariner*	Jupiter 1974
Greenhill, Basil	*The Archaeology of the Boat*	A & C Black, London, 1976
Greenhill, Basil & Gifford, Ann	*Sailing Ships: Victorian & Edwardian from Old Photographs*	Batsford Books
Haws, Duncan	*Ships and the Sea*	Hart Davis, MacGibbon, London, 1976
Hazell, Martin	*Sailing Barges*	Shire Publications Ltd.
HMSO (Admiralty)	*Manual of Seamanship*	HMSO 1908 (revised 1915)
Hough, Richard	*Fighting Ships*	Michael Joseph 1969
Joseph Jobe (Ed)	*The Great Age of Sail*	Edita Lausanne 1967
Jutsum, Capt. J. N.	*Knots and Splices*	The Nautical Press, Glasgow, 1926
MacGregor, David	*Fast Sailing Ships 1775–1875*	Conway 1988
MacGregor, David	*Merchant Sailing Ships 1775–1815*	Argus Books Ltd. 1980
McKee, E.	*Working Boats of Britain*	Conway Maritime Press 1983
Peter Kemp (Ed)	*The Oxford Companion to Ships and the Sea*	Oxford University Press London, New York and Melbourne
Rees, Abraham	*Rees's Naval Architecture 1816–20*	
Steel, David	*Art of Rigging 1818*	Fisher Nautical Press 1974
Van Powell, Nowland	*The American Navies of the Revolutionary War*	C. P. Putnam & Sons N.Y. 1974
Various authors	*Art and the Seafarer*	Faber & Faber 1968
Various authors	*The Law of Ships*	Nordbook, Sweden 1975
Veryan Heal	*Britain's Maritime Heritage (Museums & Maritime Collections)*	Conway Maritime Press
Williams, Guy R.	*The World of Model Ships and Boats*	Andre Deutsch 1971

Appendix 3

Glossary of Terms

Beam	Breadth of ship at widest point.
Bluff bows	Very rounded bows of some ships.
Bolster	A piece of wood usually with a rounded edge fixed to the trestletree frame to prevent the chafing of the shroud lines around the mast.
Bonnet	An additional strip of sail that can be laced to the foot of main course or fore-and-aft sails to increase their driving efficiency.
Boom	A spar at the foot of the main fore-and-aft sail. Minor booms were used to extend the square sail, these were attached to the main yards and called studding sail booms.
Bowsprit	Stepped into or onto the bow, supported by shroud lines, bobstay and martingale lines, it supports the headsails of a ship.
Braces	Attached to the ends of the yardarm to brace the sail around and trim the yard to the wind.
Bulkhead	A vertical partition athwarthships, also for divisions fore and aft.
Bulwark	The planking or woodwork wall along the side of a ship above the deck line.
Buttock	The breadth of ship where the hull rounds down to the stern.
Carvel built	A type of side planking where the edges are fitted tightly together making a smooth finish. The joints are caulked.
Cheeks or bibbs	Pieces of timber bolted to the mast on either side of a square-rigged ship to support the trestletrees.
Clinker built	A method of planking in which the lower edge of each plank overlaps the upper edge on the one below. A method normally used in small boat building.
Counter stern	The overhang of the stern abaft the rudder.
Course	The largest sails set upon all lower yards of a square rigged ship, referred to as fore course, main course etc.
Crab winch	A hand winch positioned aft on either side of a barge, used to raise and lower leeboards etc.
Crosstrees (1)	Part of the wooded frame, running athwart of the mast that supports the tops.
Crosstrees (2)	The word is sometimes used to describe both Trestle and Crosstrees which form a frame around the top mast and is left unboarded in this case.

Doubling	The area on masts where they overlap one another
Fid	A large wooden or iron wedge that goes through the heel of the topmast. The fid rests on the trestletrees preventing the mast dropping through.
Forecastle deck	Pronounced fo'c'sle — the forward deck and underpart.
Foremast	The first mast mounted nearest to the bows of a square-rigged ship.
Freeboard	The distance, measured in the centre of the ship, from waterline to deck level.
Frigate	A class of three-masted warship, fully rigged on each mast. Armed with from twenty four to thirty eight guns carried on a single gun deck. Rated 5th or 6th rate.
Futtock shroud	The section of the shroud lines from the underside of the top that connect with the mast band in some cases or the lower mast shrouds in others.
Gaffs	A spar to which the head of a four-sided fore-and-aft sail is laced and hoisted on the after side of the mast.
Gammon lashing or gammoning	A rope lashing consisting of seven or eight turns passing over the bowsprit and through a slot or hole in the stem. This was usually a cross lashing. Later in the 19th century it was replaced by a heavy metal band.
Gunwales	The plank that covers the head of the timbers around the upper sheer strake of a ship.
Hatch coamings	Sturdy boards mounted vertically around deck openings like cargo hatches to prevent water running down into the openings. These were six to ten inches high in sailing ships with good freeboard but higher on seagoing barges.
Hounds	Wooden shoulders bolted below the masthead either side of some ships without trestletrees to support the shroud top.
Hull	Body of the ship.
Jeers	Heavy tackle consisting of double or treble blocks used for hoisting the lower yards in square-rigged ships. A jeer capstan was usually situated between fore and main masts to sway up the yards.
Jib boom	This was an overlapped extension of the bowsprit held by a cap and band. This supported the fore topgallant and royal headstays and sails.
Keel	The lowest and principal timber of a wooden ship running fore and aft.
King plank	The centre plank of the ship's deck on wooden vessels.
King post	A short mast close to cargo hatches from which is worked small cargo derrick.
Leeboard	An early type of drop keel made of wood pivoted outboard each side of barges and other flat bottomed or shallow draughted sailing vessels. Said to have been developed by the Dutch.
Lubber hole	A small aperture in the top for the less brave to go through rather than climbing out via the futtock shrouds to gain the top.
Luff	The leading edge of a fore-and-aft sail.
Lugsail	A four-sided sail set on a lug or yard, used mainly in small craft.

Lutchet	A similar fitting to the tabernacle at deck level found on spritsail barges and wherries allowing the mast to be lowered.
Main mast	The centre mast of a square-rigged sailing ship.
Mast	A vertical spar set in a ship's deck to support other spars that in turn support the sails.
Mast butt	The thick end of a mast nearest the keel, or thick end of masts above the lower mast.
Mizzen mast	The name of the third, aftermost, mast of a square-rigged ship.
Mule rigged	'Mulie' mizzens, as on barges, consisted of a standard mizzen mast with conventional gaff and booms, as opposed to a sprit mizzen.
Parral	A method of keeping a yard against the mast and to facilitate the swing, raising and lowering of the yard. Wooden trucks threaded on wooden ribs lashed around the mast.
Poop deck	The stern or quarter deck.
Quoin	A large wooden wedge used under the butt end of naval cannons to obtain elevation. Superseded later by various fast thread screws mounted to the gun.
Running rigging	Ropes and cordage, usually running on pulley blocks that control the sails and spars of sailing ships.
Scuppers	These were draining holes or slots cut into the base of the deck bulwarks to drain surface water from the decks and waterways.
Sheave	The revolving wheel in a block. Made of lignum vitae or brass.
Sheer	Upward curve of deck towards bows and stern.
Sheets	Any rope that controls a sail from its lower corners.
Ship draft	Plans of ship.
Shipwrights	The ship building experts.
Snotter	Metal gear found on sprit rigged vessels consisting of a ring collar which fits over the heel of the sprit boom. It is chain-linked to the metal main mast strap. This supports the sprit boom, holding it close to the mast.
Spare	General term for timbers used in setting up the rigging and sails.
Spritsail	A large fore-and-aft four sided sail set on a sprit spar which stretched diagonally across the sail to support the peak. A typical barge rig. The name also describes a small square sail set on a yard beneath the bowsprit in a square rigged ship, introduced in the 16th century.
Standing rigging	Stout rigging ropes which are permanently set up to support the masts of sailing ships, as in the shrouds.
Stay	Part of the standing rigging of a sailing vessel which supports a mast in the fore-and-aft line. Forstays support forward and backstays from aft.
Stem	The foremost timber of a ship. It is attached to the keel.
Sternpost	The aftermost timber in the hull. It is attached to the keel and forms a fixing for the rudder.

Strakes   Each line of planking in a wooden ship.

Swimhead bow   Early type of barge bow, not unlike the wedge-shaped punt bow. Superseded by the straight stem bow.

Tabernacle   A wooden or metal trunk fitted to the deck of sailing ships supporting the heel of a mast, stepped at deck level. A fitting usually found on vessels that have to lower masts under bridges.

Timber heads   Vertical timbers rising through deck affording fixings for bulwark planking.

Tops   The platform structure fixed around the head of the lower mast that rests on the crosstrees.

Transom   Stern bulkhead. The squared off stern: sometimes vertical, often canted at an angle.

Trestletrees   Part of the wooded frame, running fore-and-aft of the mast that supports the tops.

Truck   A circular wooden cap with small sheaves fitted to the tops of masts. Used for signal flags. Can also refer to the wooden wheels of a gun carriage.

Tumble home   The amount by which the two sides of a ship are brought in towards the centreline after reaching their maximum beam.

Vang   The two ropes leading from the outer end of a gaff in fore-and-aft sails to prevent leeward sagging of sail and give more control over gaff.

Wales   An extra thickness of wood bolted to the sides of ships in positions where protection is needed.

Yards   A large wooden spar crossing, and attached to the mast horizontally to support a square sail.

Notes

Notes

Notes

Notes

Notes

Notes

Notes

Notes